THE
DIVINE
ROMANCE

THE
DIVINE
ROMANCE

*Going to God with the Longings
Only He Can Fulfill*

DEE BRIGHT

Revell

a division of Baker Publishing Group
Grand Rapids, Michigan

Published by Revell
a division of Baker Publishing Group
P.O. Box 6287, Grand Rapids, MI 49516-6287
www.revellbooks.com

Printed in the United States of America

Library of Congress Cataloging-in-Publication Data
Bright, Dee, 1945–
    The divine romance : going to God with the longings only he can fulfill / Dee Bright.
        p.   cm.
    Includes bibliographical references.
    ISBN 978-0-8007-3225-7 (pbk.)
    1. Christian women—Religious life. 2. Spirituality. I. Title.
BV4527.B7151 2008
248.8′43—dc22   2008006855

To my daughter, Kristi—

Thanks for being the most wonderful daughter
a mom could ever wish for,
and for always believing this book would happen.

Contents

Acknowledgments

Thank you, Vicki Crumpton, for your willingness to take on a new writer, and for championing this book to Revell. And thanks to Karen Steele, Cheryl Van Andel, Erin Bartels, Suzie Cross, Barb Barnes, Sheila Ingram, and the rest of the Revell team for your terrific input and direction. Each of you contributed greatly to my first book-writing adventure!

Max and Carol, without you I wouldn't be where I am today. Carol, you have always been an inspiration. In the lifetime I've known you, you've played many roles, but the most valued one is that of my most cherished friend. Max, you were the first man in my life to love and accept me exactly as I was—and you're *still* my best and favorite guy-friend. I cannot begin to put into words what the two of you mean to me.

My dear Yahweh Sisters, Judie and Pat—I love you guys. In the few short years we've been friends, you have been the wind beneath my wings and a source of strength and delight in my life.

Kristi and Steve, thank you for your love and encouragement and your incredible hospitality during the writing of this book. And for my two adorable grandsons, Grant and Blake—and the new little one on the way!

Barb, Linda, Karen, Ginny, and the rest of the amazing women in our writers group, this book wouldn't be here if not for your advice, encouragement, and prayers.

Byron McDonald and Carol Houston Gibbs, thanks for your encouragement to pursue the answers and for your part in planting the idea for this book.

Dyan Keppan Howk and Bonnie Juroe, you are the wonderful counselors who brought me out of my darkness and back into God's truth and light.

Barb Bonesteele, you are the one who, a long time ago, listened to my story and loved me anyway.

"Hilde," thank you for having the courage to confront my sin, even though back then I wasn't ready to hear it yet.

To all of you who so faithfully prayed for me and for the writing of this book . . . Thank you!

Part I

Our Needs

Know You're Not Alone

> But remember this—the wrong desires that come into your
> life aren't anything new and different. Many others have faced
> exactly the same problems before you.
>
> 1 Corinthians 10:13 TLB

A crisp breeze blew off the ocean. Waves broke on the sand with a rhythmic, gentle thunder. Sea gulls soared, their plaintive squawks a stark contrast to the sudden silence in conversation. But at that moment, I was oblivious to it all. I stopped dead in my tracks.

I couldn't believe the words I had just heard from my good friend Stephanie.

We had been walking on the beach for nearly an hour. I spent all that time agonizing, trying to muster the courage to tell Stephanie about a private and overwhelming struggle in my life. I had never shared it with anyone before. But it was time.

Stephanie and I first met as members of the same small prayer-and-share group at church and quickly became friends. As our friendship grew, we began sharing our personal concerns, agreeing upon accountability issues, and praying together. And as our friendship progressed, God began nudging me, the way he does when I'm being obstinate, to get my dark secret out in the open. He had recently blown apart my neat rationalizations and revealed to me just how black and ugly this sin really was. And now, the pain of bearing my secret alone was greater than the fear of sharing it. And he provided me with Stephanie, a caring, understanding friend. Today was the day.

The pain of bearing my secret alone was greater than the fear of sharing it.

I began. The words poured out, taking on volume and emotion as the story progressed. I avoided her gaze and focused on the sand at my feet, too embarrassed to look her in the eye. I shared with her how, from an early age, I learned to escape the disappointments and hurts and missing pieces of my life by relying on unhealthy substitutions. Blushing with the memory, I told her how I became infatuated with almost any romantic scene or character from a book, a movie, or TV. I thought about it constantly. I replayed each scene in my mind over and over. I confessed to her how these practices got a toehold in my adolescent life as fully developed fantasies, involving real and imagined men, and led me into a downward spiral of greater mistakes as an adult.

With stammering words, I spoke of the joy I lost over the years because of my almost constant preoccupations, and of the guilt and self-deprecation I felt as a consequence of my thoughts and resulting behaviors. Tears rolled down my cheeks and I averted my eyes in shame as I told her that what began as emotional escapes ultimately turned into the reality of affairs. And as I came to the hardest part, I choked up and barely got the words out—in one of those situations a family was torn apart.

Lastly, I told her, I now realized that my attempts to feel loved and valued by men had led, not to happiness and love, but to guilt, remorse, emptiness, resentment, and much of my life wasted.

Finally, the words stopped flowing. I felt a strange combination of embarrassment, relief, and fear. I was so afraid of what my "perfect" friend would think of *me*, the "nice little Christian woman." I had just dumped a bucket of "uglies" at her feet. I knew she would be shocked and disgusted. I was sure she would be repulsed and totally disappointed in me as a Christian sister. I held my breath and waited for a response.

༶

Some of you may be shocked at hearing about my transgressions. Others of you may feel my downfall is nothing compared to yours. As I look back on it now, I find it hard to believe that was really me. But I do realize it all began with a deep-seated and unfulfilled need. A need only God could meet. But I didn't understand that way back in the beginning.

My Battle

My struggle began in junior high school. But the story behind the story begins much earlier.

My biological father died when my mom was pregnant with me, so I grew up dreaming of the day I would have a daddy. I finally got one when I was ten years old, but unfortunately he had no desire to fill that role. One of my early survival skills was learning to be a people pleaser, and I vividly remember trying *everything* I knew to try to win that man over. I so desperately wanted him to love me. But because he was just not equipped for love, and because part of his brokenness evidenced itself in complete self-centeredness, I got absolute rejection instead. I cannot remember getting one kind look from him. Ever. Nor did he ever take my hand or hug me. In fact, when I wasn't being picked on mercilessly or ignored completely, I got looks from him that made me feel like I should be ashamed for being alive, not to mention for being in the house.

Needless to say, my little "Please love me, Daddy" hole grew into a yawning chasm by the time I hit my teens. And it continued to grow.

Once I discovered Perry Mason mysteries in junior high, I became a voracious reader. I plowed through every volume I could get my hands on and couldn't wait to get the next one. Being quite the reader herself, my mom was delighted in my newfound interest in reading. What she didn't know was that it was my anticipation of Della and Perry eventually getting together romantically that fueled my obsession. Well, that never happened, except in my fantasies.

Looking for Love

My freshman year of high school, I developed an infatuation with one of my teachers. He was oblivious, of course, or maybe he knew and was just a very kind man. Now, as an adult, it's obvious to me that I was still looking to a father figure for love. But for me at the time, it was an experience in burgeoning romance—in my head, anyway.

Many of us can identify with the character in this story:

Once upon a time there was a little girl who wanted to feel like a princess. She had dress-up princess clothes and a little princess tiara, but she still didn't *feel* like a princess. She read princess stories and dreamed of a fairy-tale prince, but she still didn't *feel* like a princess. She had little princess slippers and practiced her princess smile, but she still didn't *feel* like a princess. Every day she would look in the mirror and say to herself, "I look like a princess and act like a princess, so why don't I *feel* like a princess?" Then she figured it out. In order to feel like a princess, she needed a prince. And she's been looking for him ever since.

And aren't we all!

I accepted Christ as my Savior when I was seventeen, but I still thought and acted like a wounded, abandoned child. Inside I wanted to feel like a princess, so I desperately reached out to anything that might help me feel like one. What I didn't know for many, many years was that there is more than one way to be a princess. You can marry the fantasy fairy-tale prince, or you can be the daughter of the glorious King! Little did I know that God would be the one and only Man who would ever make me feel like a princess.

Little did I know that God would be the one and only Man who would ever make me feel like a princess.

But much more was to happen before then.

As I grew older, I became more proficient and elaborate in my fantasies. They briefly took a backseat during the early years of my marriage, but once the hope for love and happiness wore away, the fantasies returned. They were certainly better than my real life, which was growing increasingly painful. Unfortunately, the issues of emotional abandonment that I experienced in my younger years were repeated in my marriage. So, after ten years of effort and off-and-on marriage counseling, I divorced and went off on my own, along with my four-year-old daughter.

The Affair

My fantasies soon took a turn for the worse. I became infatuated with my boss, a married man with children. The familiar pattern began. First, I began indulging myself in the thought of being involved with him. Then I began creating and re-creating very realistic romantic scenarios in my mind that served to fire up my passions and make me feel the way I so desperately wanted to feel—loved and desired. Soon I began to orchestrate situations at work that on the surface seemed innocent enough. However, my motives were anything but. The odd thing is, I somehow rationalized it all.

Then, because I was able to create situations where our behavior could be compromised—it was. We began an ongoing affair, and it continued until it was discovered and brought out in the open. It was an utterly humiliating experience. But far beyond the embarrassment and disgrace was what it did to my boss and his family. Because of our affair, he lost his job and his family was destroyed.

Talking about it now makes my heart ache and brings to mind Paul's words, I am the "worst of sinners" (see 1 Timothy 1:15–16). I know I'm forgiven, but I can do nothing to change the reality of the consequences.

The Downward Spiral

Logic would dictate that I would learn from this horrific lesson. But I didn't. It was as if there was a separate person living inside me. On the exterior I appeared to be a nice, wholesome, and moral person. And I *felt* that way. I wasn't pretending. But on the inside something insidious had taken over. My obsession to feel okay about myself could be satiated only by attracting and winning the attention and "love" of a man. I made mistake after mistake. I was still going to church, reading my Bible, and praying. But the blinders were so securely attached that I literally could not see the sin. It makes no sense, I know. But it also demonstrates that when we give ourselves to sin, we can no longer trust our conscience.

As I look back on all this, I am so incredibly grateful to God that he somehow protected me from making further devastating mistakes with married men, some with kids. I know he was protecting those wives and children too.

The Beast

In the midst of this black and despicable time in my life, one of the guys in my Bible study group told me about his Adult Children of Alcoholics group. For a reason I don't remember now, I decided to go. It was moderately interesting, and I picked up a few pieces of material as I left. Later that evening I began reading the information and a strange thing happened.

I recognized myself.

I was dumbfounded. I was reading about people with *addictions*, and they were describing me.

I felt like I had been hit by lightning. The more I read, the more irrefutable the facts became. I was struggling with a full-blown, had-me-by-the-neck, cruel, evil addiction. And it was leering back at me with a malevolent grin.

I was reading about people with addictions, and they were describing me.

The blinders were ripped away. My eyes were opened.

Suddenly I saw it the way God saw it: black, slimy, repulsive, insidious, loathsome, horrific, and vile.

It was also powerful, malicious, resolute, and tenacious. In the ensuing months of my battle, I came to call it The Beast.

This was the struggle I shared with my friend Stephanie that day on the beach.

Stephanie stopped walking. My heart was racing, dreading what she might say next. I braced myself when she turned to me and spoke.

"You know, I've struggled with very much the same thing."

I was stunned! No awkward silence. No false words in an attempt to sound understanding. No rebuke. Instead, she shared some of her own pain. She had made mistakes too. Her stumbles were different than mine, but they shared the same origin—the desire to fill an aching, longing, empty space deep inside. She understood. I wasn't alone! And for the first time in my life, I felt free of my secret.

Now, to fully appreciate the significance of this moment, you have to understand a little something about Stephanie. She is one of those truly admirable people. She is incredibly funny and can be outrageous at times. She is intelligent, tremendously creative, caring, and thoughtful, yet one of the humblest people I know. But her most attractive quality is that she's an awesome Christian woman, totally committed to her walk with God. And this brings me to my point: not in a million years would I have dreamed that Stephanie—wonderful, sweet, exemplary Stephanie—ever struggled with the same yearnings and temptations as I did.

The Journey Begins

That morning on the beach was only the beginning. My road to recovery was long and hard-fought. But God is faithful, and he walked every inch of that road with me. Best of all, he forgives me. I have to live with the consequences of my sin, but he graciously and patiently forgives the sin. In 1 Timothy 1:15–16, Paul says, "Christ Jesus came into the world to save sinners—of whom I am the worst. But for that very reason I was shown mercy so that in me, the worst of sinners, Christ Jesus might display his unlimited patience as an example for those who would believe on him and receive eternal life."

No matter how badly we mess up, God's patience is unlimited!

So, if you're hiding something dark inside, fearing it's unforgivable, remember Paul's words. No matter how badly we mess up, God's patience is unlimited!

From time to time I have to remind myself of his forgiveness and grace—especially as I put this on paper for the first time. I am no longer the same person. God has performed a "renewing of my mind," and I am now free from the bondage of that sin. But like a recovering alcoholic, I know how important it is not to take that first drink. In my case, it's the drink of fantasy. My rule now is to "take captive every thought to make it obedient to Christ" (2 Corinthians 10:5). The moment my mind entertains the slightest notion of fantasizing, I must grab that thought and present it to God. No hesitation.

I'm sharing this with you in the hope that you will see that where there is *longing*, there is something bigger and deeper.

Real Feelings, Real Desires

That day marked a fresh beginning for me. Until that moment, I didn't believe other women had the same wrong desires I did, at least not women in the Christian community. Boy, was I wrong!

Not long after my walk on the beach with Stephanie, I began to get a little bolder. One evening following our Saturday night church service, I went to dinner with a few of my single female friends. After ordering our meals, our conversation quickly turned to other things: the sermon, our diets, hot social issues, and, inevitably . . . men. We had just settled into our modest repast of fresh green salads, garlic cheese toast, and pasta when the topic veered to the feelings we had about being single.

This was my chance! I wanted to go deeper into this unexplored terrain. And I knew that as I became more comfortable sharing my own struggle, it would hold less power over me. Still, it was a scary proposition. I looked around the table at these three godly women. Tentatively, I began.

I believe I blurted out something along these lines: "I really struggle with my romantic and sexual thoughts and feelings about men." I paused here to assess the reaction. Noting Elena's raised eyebrows and a bit of facial paralysis but no out-and-out shock with Rebecca or Jennifer, I valiantly continued.

21

"I've been going through a major battle with my thought life. God has been showing me—in no uncertain ways—that allowing myself to fantasize about guys is wrong. And in the past, it has led to trouble for me. But this is something that has become an ingrained habit in order to feel okay about myself, and it's really hard to deal with when I feel so untouched and unloved in my life."

Silence.

In an offhand manner, and in hopes that someone would change the subject or rescue me from this rapidly deepening pit into which I was digging myself, I made a sweeping motion toward my friends around the table and said, "Maybe I'm the only one who . . . ," and before I could finish my sentence, I witnessed vigorously shaking heads all around, and all three women began talking at once.

Married and Single

The conversation that followed was both animated and thoughtful. Rebecca, a single mom, openly and honestly began to share her frustrations with being alone and with not having physical affection. Quiet, smiling, and sensitive, Rebecca is the essence of Christian femininity. And she's struggling with all the challenges any mother of a teenage son faces.

Jennifer brought up how hurt she felt being excluded from social life with married couples at church. Now here is a brave woman. Jennifer is a single woman in her thirties who decided to go back to school full-time for a degree in family counseling. Which also means homework, an almost full-time job, living on a shoestring budget, and very little discretionary time. She is gifted as a speaker, counselor, nurturing friend, and cook.

Elena lamented about how difficult it seemed to meet single, Christ-focused, emotionally healthy men in our particular age groups. Snatched by God from her self-professed "wild" lifestyle, Elena is now a woman deeply committed to purity and to discovering all that God has for her life. With Elena, you never know what to expect. One moment you're in awe of an incredibly profound insight she has shared. The next, you're holding your ribs in gales of laughter after hearing a hilarious family story, complete with Elena mimicking her mother's German accent.

And, as the dinner progressed, we eventually spoke about how we wrestled with what the world has to offer as substitutes for genuine love and feelings of self-worth. As Elena put it, "There's just so much out there you can indulge in if you let yourself."

That's when Jennifer brought up an important fact: "You know, it's not just about being single. Married women have these same problems." She then launched into a story about a friend who had discovered that marriage was nothing like she had expected it to be. "My friend hinted that instead of the deep, emotionally rewarding relationship she had envisioned, hers turned out to be a 'routine and mundane life, totally without romance or spontaneity.' And she feels she mostly spends it alone."

"I have a Christian friend at work in the same boat," Elena added. "She feels her husband treats her more like a sexual object than a wife or friend. It seems that the only time he shows any real interest in her at all is when he's interested in sex. She feels used and rejected. And trapped in her marriage."

"My friend Sarah is married to a great guy, but she says even he can't always make her feel the way she wants to feel," Rebecca continued. "She says a guy just can't be everything a woman expects him to be."

Each of us felt most of our married friends had similar stories. And we acknowledged that many of them struggled with wanting to feel loved and valued, just like us.

"So what's the answer?" we all wanted to know. As we continued to talk, and we brought God's love for us into the picture, we agreed that humans are just too human to be completely selfless all the time. And we also agreed that only

God is capable of completely and unconditionally loving us, and that he alone can know exactly what each of us needs.

We reached a significant conclusion that evening. We had somehow assumed that a man in our lives would meet our needs of "just wanting to feel loved." But we now knew the hard truth, and here it is: no man can meet all of our needs, yours and mine. Only God can fill our empty, yearning places inside. Only he can make us feel whole. Only his love can make us feel adored and cherished the way we really, really want to be adored and cherished.

Only God can fill our empty, yearning places inside. Only he can make us feel whole.

And we also knew that just *knowing* and acknowledging this truth didn't make the feelings change and didn't make the temptations go away.

As we finally pushed back from the table and began to gather our things to leave the restaurant, Rebecca said, "This is really good. We need to be talking about these things more often. Why haven't we talked about all of this before?"

And the resounding response was, "NO ONE talks about it! Pastors don't. Women don't. Books don't."

Well, this book does! Single or married, as you move through the chapters that follow, you'll have an opportunity to consider how to balance your genuine, unmet needs, feelings, and desires with God's best for your life. If you've ever felt dissatisfied or incomplete, and believed that the right kind of man could meet those needs, then this is the book for you. If you've ever felt that you're not lovable enough, beautiful enough, worthy enough, or talented enough to be really loved, then you'll appreciate that you are not alone! And if you ever yearn to feel more cherished, adored, accepted, and valued than you do right now, read on. You'll realize in a new, fresh, and very practical way how you can experience God more personally and intimately, and how you can allow him to love you with a passion you've never imagined!

Embrace the Adventure!

I encourage you to write in this book—fill the margins with your reactions, thoughts, questions, feelings, and insights. Highlight things that jump off the page for you. Do the exercises. Answer the questions. Accept the "Challenge!" at the end of each chapter and "Involve God in Your Resolve" to seek his clarity, his will, and his abundance for you—his child, his daughter.

At the end of the book, we will look at information and tools that will enable us to live victorious, no-compromise lives. And as part of our wrap-up, you'll have an opportunity to formulate your own Personal Action Plan. Take advantage of the exercises, and put your passions on paper where you can review and track your progress.

So, join me as we jump into the fray. *Embrace the adventure* of living your life *fully* with the internal, abiding joy God intends for you!

Chapter Summary

Step 1: Know You're Not Alone

1. Remember that many other women struggle with their unmet needs from men, just like you, but they probably don't talk about it.
2. Recognize there may be battles to overcome, but that God is more powerful than Satan.
3. Let God begin where you are right now.

Challenge!

Jot down your responses to the questions below. If you are concerned about writing them here, create a loose-leaf notebook or purchase a journal and keep it in a safe place.

1. What do you hope will happen for you as you read through the remainder of this book?

_____

_____

_____

_____

2. Are you willing to look at how God desires for you to live your life, in spite of how difficult it might seem? Why or why not?

_____

_____

_____

_____

3. What one, specific thing do you want to do differently in your life as it relates to dealing with unmet needs? What are you willing to do differently *this week*?

_____

_____

_____

Involve God in Your Resolve!

Seek God's clarity, his will, and his abundance for you—his child, his daughter.

> *Abba, Daddy, I know that you are the Giver of every good and perfect gift. Thank you that you love me so much that you were willing to give your Son for me. I love you and I desire to live my life the way you want me to live it. There are areas in my life where I am hurting. I have had people and circumstances disappoint me. My life has not always been the way I imagined it would be. Show me how I am trying to fill the empty places in my life in the wrong ways. Forgive me for seeking my fulfillment from people and circumstances instead of looking to you to meet those needs. Father, I need you and your strength to succeed, and I thank you that you are here for me! As it says in Psalm 119:33–35, "Just tell me what to do and I will do it, Lord. As long as I live I'll wholeheartedly obey. Make me walk along the right paths for I know how delightful they really are" (TLB).*

What else do you want to ask God right now? What else do you want to tell him?

_____

_____

_____

_____

_____

> *I pray this in the name of your precious Son, Jesus. Amen.*

27

What do you sense he is saying to you right now?

_____

_____

_____

_____

Step 2

Admit Your Unmet Needs

What has been will be again, what has been done will be done again; there is nothing new under the sun.

Ecclesiastes 1:9

After our conversation around the dinner table that evening, I became more determined to find answers. Married or single, what are we as Christian women supposed to do with all of these deep, unfulfilled desires? And how does our relationship with God fit into the solution of the problem? If he requires purity—"You must be holy because I am holy" (1 Peter 1:16 NLT)—then what's okay for me and what's not? Is it permissible for me to think about whatever I want to think about, as long as I don't act on my thoughts? Can I indulge in reading materials or movies that make me feel good as long as it doesn't go any further? And, after all, the Bible isn't specific when talking about two unmarried consenting adults, is it? Or is it? If I feel that my life circumstances have dealt me a bad hand, isn't it my right to look for alternate ways to meet my needs? God doesn't want me to be unhappy, does he? Good questions. And we'll answer them. We will also discuss some of the common pitfalls lurking out there in the world. And we'll deal in depth with the issue of God's benchmark for holiness and purity.

After that landmark dinner, I began reading copiously. I plowed through the Scriptures. I talked to pastors. I spent time discussing these issues with a small circle of intimate female friends. All the while, I was still struggling. I was learning and growing, but still struggling.

One day my search led me to talk with our director of women's ministry. I shared with her about my quest and some of my discoveries. I talked about my yet unanswered questions. And I mentioned that this seemed to be a topic of considerable interest. I told her I had gathered a great deal of worthwhile information that needed somehow to be shared. "We should offer this as a workshop for single women at our upcoming women's retreat," she agreed. I suggested the name of "Ahh . . . Men!" and she loved it. So it stuck.

Now you must understand that in spite of my twenty-some years as a professional trainer and facilitator, this was a scary proposition. It would mean being vulnerable with a group of unfamiliar people. Would anyone even show up? After all, the workshop topic was a bit sensitive. I did, however, believe that God wanted me to share what I had learned so far.

I immersed myself in the task. How could I put all this newly acquired information into forty-five minutes? And what did I hope each woman would get out of our time together? I prayed, did more research, and was finally ready. Well, as ready as I could be!

The Ahh . . . Men! Seminar Is Born

Our retreat was located in the beautiful mountains near Lake Arrowhead, just two hours from Los Angeles. It was Day Two, and so far everything had been wonderful. The keynote speaker was marvelous and insightful. The meals were great, but of course I have only one criterion for "good food": that someone else fixes it!

Not knowing what to expect in the way of attendance for my workshop, we had reserved a small room in the conference center. As the space completely filled and even more women arrived, we had to start tucking chairs into nooks and corners of the little room. Finally, we were ready to begin.

The first exercise asked the workshop participants to respond to two sets of questions:

> *What am I supposed to do with all these feelings?*

1. What are the feelings we sometimes experience as a result of being single, alone? What are some of the unmet needs we have?
2. Would being married meet these needs and resolve the feelings? What would some married women say?

Before getting them started, I shared an excerpt from my own journal:

> God, why did you make me the way you did? You *knew* what my life circumstances were going to be, so why did you create me as an affectionate person? I could have been one of those cold types that don't have a high need to give and receive physical affection, who doesn't need or want close companionship. But instead you loaded me down with all these desires to be close to someone and to share my life with someone. And then you decided to let me live my life alone. It doesn't make sense and it doesn't seem fair. What am I supposed to do with all these feelings?

Having said that, I asked the participants to get into small groups of three or four, and then turned them loose for ten minutes of discussion. When time was up, I stood ready at my flip chart, hoping and praying that I would get more than just superficial answers.

Wow! Was I surprised! It was as if we'd wrenched open the main valve on a fire hydrant. "I feel so unloved and untouched." "I wish it wasn't always just me to get everything done at home." "I want someone to sit in bed and read the morning paper with me." The responses filled page after page on the flip chart. Their thoughts were tinged with emotions—sadness, anger, disappointment, despair. "Since my husband died, I'm lonely all the time." "I don't see any guys out there close to what I want." "I'm forty-two and still single. Will there ever be someone for me?" Women began throwing out specific topics they hoped we would be able to address during our time together. "So, what am I supposed to do with all my feelings?" "Will we talk about self-gratification?" "Will we get a list of what's okay to do and what's not?" The intensity of their interest was overwhelming.

And when our time was up, so many wanted more. They, too, asked the question my friend Rebecca had asked in the restaurant months before. "Why aren't there more opportunities to discuss these relevant issues?" "How come we never hear answers to these concerns from the pulpit?" And, "We need more time to discuss all this. When can we get together again?"

Well, that seminar led to more seminars, for single *and* married women. We have talked, cried, and laughed together. Some women are faced with very unique situations. Most of us have a lot in common. Some women are divorced, and some are widowed. Some women have never been married. Some are married yet are so unfulfilled they are wishing they weren't. Some are happily married but still experiencing a vague emptiness inside.

Nothing New Under the Sun

This whole issue of wanting to feel loved and desired and attractive is nothing new. It's been around since the beginning of time. Women want the affection and attentions of a man.

They want to experience romance. They want to feel singularly adored, special, and beautiful. Nothing has changed.

Now granted, back in Old Testament times women weren't constantly made to feel inferior by being bombarded with images of perfect, beautiful women plastered on large billboards down at the city well. But, married and single, they had challenges of their own. Let's go back in time . . .

This whole issue of wanting to feel loved and desired and attractive is nothing new.

It is long before the Ten Commandments made their debut. You're a middle-aged married woman, and you love your husband, Fred. One afternoon Mr. Husband comes home and announces, "Look, honey! I've found us a gorgeous, shapely young babe to help us make even more babies! I'm sure you and Bambi-sha will get along just fine!"

Ouch! Can you imagine how that felt?

But let's not overlook the predicament of unmarried women in those times. As a young, single maiden, you spend most of your time with your family but on occasion go to the marketplace or the well. And lately you've noticed this cute, lithe, buff Adonis casting smiles and surreptitious glances your way. Your little heart is aflutter as you make your way home with your basket full of fruit and your head full of possibilities. Imagine your surprise as you open the front door to find two grinning parents and a large, hairy stranger. "Surprise, sweetheart! We've just betrothed you to Gronk the goat herder. He smells bad, but he's a great provider!"

Real Women

We don't have to look very far in the Bible to see real women with real feelings, disappointments, and hurts. In Genesis we read the story of Jacob, Leah, and Rachel (see Genesis 29:15–35). Jacob loved Rachel and worked seven years for her father in order to win her hand in marriage. But her father tricked him, and he found himself married to Leah, Rachel's older sister. Shortly thereafter, and with a promise to work another seven years, he also took Rachel as his wife.

We are told that "Jacob . . . loved Rachel more than Leah" (v. 30). Can you put yourself in Leah's shoes and feel how she must have felt? God did. "When the LORD saw that Leah was not loved, he opened her womb" (v. 31) and allowed her to have children. A woman's value in those days was tied to her ability to produce children, especially heirs. Yet, in spite of this honor of bearing Jacob's firstborn son, we see Leah's broken heart. In biblical times a child's name reflected circumstances surrounding the birth. In spite of the joy that must have accompanied this new little boy, Leah named him Reuben because, she said, "The LORD has seen my misery. Surely my husband will love me now" (v. 32). When her second son was born, she named him Simeon, a name which again reflected her lamentable situation: "Because the LORD heard that I am not loved, he gave me this one too" (v. 33).

Just as God's heart ached for those women and their disappointments, his heart aches for us.

How sad. I'm sure Old Testament women found ways to deal with their disappointments and pain. Maybe they did their best to bury their feelings. Or perhaps they acted on them. Or it's likely they, too, chose substitutions, just as we sometimes do. They weren't tempted by a stash of romance novels artfully concealed in their cooking pots. They didn't have access to titillating conversations in Inter-hut chat rooms. But they most likely had some means of creating comfort for themselves or for masking their pain. It's possible they fell into some of the same traps we face today—fantasy, gossip, flirtation, lust, affairs.

Just as God's heart ached for those women and their disappointments, his heart aches for us. Just as his heart grieved over their sinful choices, his heart grieves over ours.

Our lives don't always turn out the way we anticipate. We end up in marriages that don't seem to satisfy our deeper needs. Or as single women, we find ourselves all alone. As I discovered in the workshops, most of us are looking for more.

Ah, but That's Only the Beginning!

This book grew out of those Ahh . . . Men! workshops. And the workshops were the impetus behind further research and a deeper desire to apply what I've learned to my own life. Easier said than done.

I'm convinced God has a sense of humor. Just about the time we think we have our act together (chuckle, chuckle), he shines the light somewhere else. I heard a good story a number of years ago that provides an excellent illustration.

During World War II, Allied troops had established a beachhead on one of the South Pacific islands, thus claiming "authority" over the island. But now that the troops had landed, the island needed to be made safe. There were numerous caves on the island, and many enemy soldiers were still hiding there in the darkness. So the Allied troops had their work cut out for them. One cave at a time, they would shine their lights into the interior, exposing anyone hiding within. Once that cave was safely cleared, they would then move on to the next. One by one, each cave was examined until, after much time, the entire island was declared under their control.

You're probably already guessing the analogy. When we accept Christ as our Savior, he establishes his "beachhead" in us. He lays claim to us. We become his. But we still have a whole "island" full of dark caves that are hiding our sins, our deceits, our weaknesses. Proverbs 20:27 tells us, "The Lord's light penetrates the human spirit, exposing every hidden motive" (NLT). God doesn't tackle all the caves at once. Instead, just like the soldiers in the South Pacific, he shines his light into one cave at a time.

I'm a little slow with this concept. Every time I experience a victory in my walk with God, I'm doing the *Rocky* dance—jogging around my living room, arms high above my head. I'm thinking I'm finally arriving at that comfortable, spiritually mature place. Not!

Before I'm even done celebrating, God is there with his flashlight, poking around in another one of my caves.

The Good News

In spite of the disappointing realization that I will never be perfect as long as I'm walking here on earth, there is some good news. I'm learning. I'm recognizing that at the *root* of the sin in most of my caves there is an unmet need or an unrealistic expectation.

And now I'm beginning to better understand how God wants me to deal with those unfulfilled needs. It's a matter of putting into practice what I know. It's about changing old habits—and old "habits of thought"—on a day-to-day, moment-by-moment basis. It's about living to glorify him rather than to please myself. It's a daunting task, but the rewards for the occasional victories are sweet! And God doesn't expect me to do it perfectly or to do it all by myself. Over and over we are told in his Word that he is always with us, always available to help us.

God doesn't expect me to do it perfectly or to do it all by myself.

I love Philippians 4:13 as translated in the Living Bible: "For I can do everything God asks me to with the help of Christ who gives me the strength and power." When I struggle, Isaiah 41:10 encourages me with, "So do not fear, for I am with you; do not be dismayed, for I am your God. I will strengthen you and help you; I will uphold you with my righteous right hand." And no matter how often I fail, I am reminded that I can be "confident of this, that he who began a good work in [me] will carry it on to completion until the day of Christ Jesus" (Philippians 1:6).

I am still passionate about this pursuit of putting aside poor and sinful substitutes for the real joy God can provide, in spite of the neediness I'm experiencing. And there are actually real and very practical solutions for this challenge. God did not design the world to be the way it is today, but we're living in it. So I continue to search, to explore, to research, to ask questions, and to read. I want the answers as much for myself as I want them for others.

Let Us Run with Perseverance

That day on the beach with Stephanie was only the beginning. God had much, much more in store for me. And I am confident that he has much more in store for you! We have life. We have *true* life in Christ. And he came that we might experience life with more abundance (see John 10:10).

The Christian walk is not for wimps or wimpettes. Once you begin the journey, you discover it is the greatest challenge there is in this world. We're up against some pretty impressive obstacles, and we need to be in constant readiness.

As we have discussed in these first two chapters, our feelings and unmet needs sometimes get in the way, and we need to know how to recognize them and deal with them in a healthy, constructive way. The way we interpret events and personal interactions has a powerful impact on how we react or respond to the people and circumstances around us. The prevailing worldview and our culture are both determined to pull us down to their level. Our "old nature"

The Christian walk is not for wimps or wimpettes. Once you begin the journey you discover it is the greatest challenge there is in this world.

is constantly warring against God's Spirit in us, playing on every human desire and weakness to convince us to give in to what it wants. And then of course, there is Satan, the great deceiver and the father of lies. That "roaring lion," as he is described in the Bible, wants nothing more than to have us live our lives in mediocrity, or worse. We need to be aware and be prepared in order to successfully live our lives as free women in Christ, not as "slaves" to our opponents. We will cover all of this as we continue to progress through the book together.

And because we need to make intelligent, committed choices, we will take a realistic look at the *cost* of living our lives God's way—*and* the cost of ignoring God and doing it our way! It's at this point we will lay out the practical steps for victory over our old, negative thoughts and behaviors.

As we move through the chapters ahead, you will be challenged! I encourage you to not give up but to "run with perseverance the race marked out for us. Let us fix our eyes on Jesus, the *author* and *perfecter* of our faith" (Hebrews 12:1–2, emphasis mine). Let's allow him to correct and cultivate us as we walk with him. And we can know that, like the loving, watchful, fully involved Daddy he is, he'll be right there with us, every step of the way.

Chapter Summary

Step 2: Admit Your Unmet Needs

1. Accept that unmet needs have been a reality for a long time.
2. Let God shine his light in your "caves," one at a time.
3. Trust God to meet the needs that no man can—no matter how wonderful he is!

Challenge!

1. What are some of your unmet needs? Where are you hurting or feeling unfulfilled? Whether you're married or single, what is it you want or expect from a man in your life?

_____

_____

_____

_____

2. What are you hiding in some of your "caves"? How are you attempting to fill or "dull" your unmet needs? (Examples: reading material, excessive work, movies, staying busy, fantasy, eating, etc.)

_____

_____

_____

_____

3. Specifically, how do you want God to help you?

_____

_____

_____

_____

Involve God in Your Resolve!

Ask God to show you where he desires to see you grow.

Father, thank you that you love me and desire to meet my every need. I know that looking for solutions apart from you won't bring me lasting joy. As I begin this adventure of exploring my unmet needs, walk with me, stay close beside me. Your Word tells me that you both precede me and follow me, and place your hand of blessing on my head (Psalm 139:5). I know I won't be alone. Reveal to me your perfect will for my life. Shine your light where there is darkness. Clarify things when I am confused. Lead me on your path of everlasting life. I want to delight you in all I do.

What else do you want to ask God right now? What else do you want to tell him?

_____

_____

_____

_____

_____

I pray this in the name of your precious Son, Jesus. Amen.

What do you sense he is saying to you right now?

_____

_____

_____

======= Step 3 =======

Manage Your Feelings

We are not masters of our own feeling, but we are by God's grace masters of our consent.

St. Francis de Sales

Since that evening around the dinner table several years ago, I discovered, in fact, that *many* women struggle with male-related feelings. Feelings that pull and tug and demand some sort of placation. Many of these emotions stem from wrong beliefs. And many of these beliefs are rooted in old hurts.

Now, we're not going to attempt to address the deep psychological implications of how our past impacts our present. Nor will we deal with specific dysfunctional attitudes and behaviors. What we will do is talk about some of the *feelings* that emanate from the false beliefs we've collected over the years. We are complicated creations. Emotionally, mentally, physically, and spiritually. And that's a *good* thing! But from that complexity come complex feelings.

On any day, we may encounter a wide range of emotions: joy, sadness, happiness, contentment, loneliness, resentment, excitement, and so on. Many of us carry around a backpack of *old* hurts that weigh us down with feelings of unforgiveness, anger, self-pity, fear, or distrust. We may have feelings *stacked* on feelings. So what are we supposed to do with them?

Feelings Are Real, and They're Healthy

For starters, we must acknowledge that it's okay to have feelings—God built us that way. And God doesn't make mistakes. The very feelings we've been discussing—the need for love, sex, intimacy, companionship—are normal. God made man, and then he made woman. He designed them to be drawn to each other. This physical attraction between man and woman was—and is—a God-given, natural magnetism.

It's okay to have feelings — God built us that way.

Just imagine Adam in the garden. God has formed every beast of the field and every bird of the air and brought them to Adam to see what he would call them (see Genesis 2:19). So Adam has spent hours and hours thinking up all these great names for things, like gnu, wildebeest, ichneumon, gerbil, and such. No wonder he slept so peacefully while God removed one of his ribs! When he wakes up, groggy from his nap, there is Eve, his counterpart and helpmate. He rubs his still-sleepy eyes in disbelief at this marvelous creature standing before him. As the fog clears, his eyes open wide, and he says with amazement, "WHOOOAA!! MAAAN!!" (A phonetic rendering later shortened to "woman.") And I'm sure Eve's first words upon seeing her mate must have been "HUBBA-HUBBA!" (This is most likely the root word for "husband.")

Pardon the literary license! The point is that we were fashioned by God to be naturally attracted to one another as men and women. And whether or not we have a husband, we're still going to have desires for intimacy, affection, and companionship.

How God Designed the World

We have to remind ourselves that God never intended for us to have unmet needs in relationships. When Adam was created, he was without sin. The same for Eve. Together they flourished in the garden. Wow! Think what it must have been like. No pretense. No games. No selfishness. No self-consciousness. Just pure love. Pure acceptance. Two people who were intimately connected. And on top of all that, they had God as an intimate friend. The three of them walked and talked together in the garden. It must have been beautiful.

In his book *In the Eye of the Storm*, Max Lucado describes what an angel might have witnessed as God walked him through history, beginning with the perfect, sinless Eden:

> The angel gasped at what he saw. Spontaneous love. Voluntary devotion. Chosen tenderness. Never had he seen anything like these. He felt the love of the Adams. He heard the joy of Eve and her daughters. He saw the food and the burdens shared. He absorbed the kindness and marveled at the warmth.
>
> "Heaven has never seen such beauty, my Lord. Truly, this is your greatest creation."[1]

The angel saw Adam and Eve as God's greatest creation because they were given a *choice*, and they were *choosing* to love and obey God. As a result, they were living in a perfect world. A world without sin. And in that brief paragraph we can envision what God intended for us as his obedient children. I'm sure in God's design no one would ever feel alone or rejected, hurt or wounded, broken or brokenhearted. But God also gave us (as humans) a choice: to obey him and delight in his love or to live the way we want to live.

When sin entered the picture, everything changed. Lucado continues his story:

> A stench enveloped the pair. The angel turned in horror and proclaimed, "What is it?"

The Creator spoke only one word: "Selfishness."

The angel stood speechless as they passed through centuries of repugnance. Never had he seen such filth. Rotten hearts. Ruptured promises. Forgotten loyalties. Children of the creation wandering blindly in lonely labyrinths.[2]

This is the world in which we now live. It's a bit different than the way it began, isn't it? But it's our reality. We're living in a fallen world. And our fallen world is full of imperfect people (including me and you, by the way!). No wonder we are inundated with not-so-great feelings. No wonder we sometimes experience such painful emotions.

So, now that we've established the reality of our feelings, what are we supposed to do with them? There are three choices.

The First Choice: If It Feels Good . . .

The world seems sold on the idea of acting on whatever passions, desires, and fantasies we might experience. Just look at soaps as an example. There seems to be no connection between the physical urges of the characters and the thinking parts of their brains.

Randomly pick up a women's magazine at the checkout counter and be amazed at the advice. We are encouraged to "give in to and explore" our fantasies in order to fully realize and develop ourselves. Many articles suggest having an affair to raise our consciousness and confidence.

Have you noticed that in most sitcoms the first passionate kiss is almost always followed immediately by sex? If we are not shown a humorous in-bed bit after the fact, we are told about it as the characters unabashedly share this information with their friends.

The world's way is quite different from what the Bible teaches us. It is no surprise, then, that in movies, TV, and the media in general, the *consequences* of acting on wrong desires are often glossed over. In reality the consequences of giving in to our emotions and desires often hurt others and ultimately hurt us.

The feelings we have are normal. But if they lead us into inappropriate or sinful thoughts and behaviors, then they are not to be dwelled on or acted upon. When we settle for short-term gratification, we are losing out on God's long-term blessings in our lives.

> *When we settle for short-term gratification, we are losing out on God's long-term blessings in our lives.*

The Second Choice: Don't Feel That Way

Another approach to dealing with our feelings is to deny them. While this may seem like a good short-term fix, in the long term, it's not. Our feelings are real, so it's best to acknowledge them as real. What we do with our feelings, however, is another matter.

Unfortunately, in some Christian circles, we may be told that certain feelings are wrong. Well-intentioned friends may try to minimize or negate our emotions. I agree with Elisabeth Elliot when she states, "Do not debunk feelings *as such*. Remember they are given to us as part of our humanity. Do not try to fortify yourself *against* emotions."[3]

So where does that leave us?

The Third—and *Best*—Choice

Let's finish Elisabeth's thought as she prescribes our third, and healthier, option: "Recognize [your emotions]; name them, if that helps; and then lay them open before the Lord for His training of your responses. The discipline of emotions is the training of responses."[4]

Hear that? Recognize those feelings. Then lay them before the Lord! Let him help you with them. They're real. Don't let anyone tell you they're not. God created feelings to keep us in touch with ourselves and with our world.

Now, I'm not suggesting that just because feelings are a normal and healthy part of our lives that we wallow in them. Like inappropriate thoughts, ungodly feelings need to be acknowledged but also dealt with correctly. A sinful thought is not sinful. Thoughts often pop into our heads unbidden; *dwelling* on the sinful thought is sinful! Having a sinful feeling come over us is normal and not a sin; *luxuriating* in it, however, is.

"You can't keep a bird from landing on your head, but you can keep it from building a nest in your hair."

Here's a great saying: "You can't keep a bird from landing on your head, but you can keep it from building a nest in your hair."

Acknowledge your feelings as being real for you. It is important to feel what we feel, to understand what we are feeling, and if possible, to get to the root of why we are feeling what we're feeling. Very often, there's much more below the surface.

Icebergs and Emotions

It's a scientific fact that only about 10 percent of an iceberg is usually seen above the surface of the ocean. There's another 90 percent of the monstrous iceberg lurking below. This is often the case with our emotions. What we are actually experiencing is only the top layer of the real problem. What is consciously obvious to us is only the very tip of the iceberg!

Let me give you an example.

Angie is always cheerful. She bends over backwards for others. I had never seen Angie angry. One day Angie called me to chat. In the course of our conversation it became apparent that she was feeling very angry toward one of our mutual single friends, Sam. When I asked her what Sam had done to make her so angry, she replied, "He showed up twenty minutes late to help me stack boxes in my garage!"

Hmmm. Sounded like the pointy part of an iceberg to me. I inquired, "Sooo, you sound pretty upset about Sam being late. But if he was being nice enough to come over and help you, why would you be so upset about that?"

She went on to tell me about all the times she had helped Sam with things and that she was always on time. After all, she valued Sam as a friend, and being on time was a way of demonstrating respect.

Okay. I agreed with that. But maybe there was more to this . . .

"So, you feel Sam was being disrespectful of you?"

"Yes! I mean, if he cared about me at all . . ."

Okay, now we were getting somewhere. I let her go on for a moment and then said, "You *like* Sam, don't you." It was a statement, not a question.

I swear I could hear her blushing on the other end of the line!

As we continued our conversation, we uncovered the following: Angie secretly was interested in Sam. As a result, she was weighing and measuring his every action and word to determine if the feelings were mutual. She thought they might be. That is, until he showed up late. With that one offense, Angie assumed Sam wasn't interested. And that hurt her feelings. Okay, now we're slightly below the waterline. You might think we'd found the real issue, but . . .

Let's go deeper. As we talked, we realized that her perception of Sam not being interested made Angie feel "not good enough, not attractive enough, not, not, not." You get the picture. Now we were definitely submerged.

The real kicker came when Angie said, "My dad was the same way. I could never count on him for anything."

Bingo! Now we had touched on some of Angie's deeper issues. And we were probably somewhere near the base of the iceberg.

So let's recap. The tip of Angie's iceberg looked like anger. As we dove below the surface, we found hurt, then unworthiness, and then unmet needs from Dad. There was a lot more to this iceberg than met the eye.

Holes and Hurts

None of us have come through our lives unscathed. We all have old baggage of some kind. As kids, we each employed some way of avoiding hurt from others. It may have been laughing when we felt others were being unkind to us. It may have been zoning out or fantasizing—mentally moving ourselves somewhere else so we didn't have to experience pain. It may have been pulling away or avoiding—if we can't be seen, we can't be hurt. It may have been fighting back. Whatever we did, it worked for us at the time and helped us to survive.

Many of us are no longer in touch with ourselves.

Unfortunately, when we employ these same strategies as adults, they hinder rather than help us. Some of these behaviors have become automatic reactions we employ in order to dull or avoid our pain. Many are self-defeating. Most of them are nonproductive habitual responses to uncomfortable feelings and circumstances. But rather than beat ourselves up because of them, we can learn to recognize them for what they are—coping mechanisms. They helped us *survive* as children, so we very naturally fall into those same strategies when we experience similar feelings now. We're simply trying to "stop the pain."

Most of these coping approaches have taught us to separate ourselves from what we are really feeling. As a result, many of us are no longer in touch with ourselves. The feelings might simply present themselves as big, invisible, heavy, uncomfortable "clouds" that weigh on us. We can't define them; we just know we don't like them.

Get In Touch

Several years ago while talking with my counselor, I learned about icebergs personally. During the course of discussion, I admitted feeling angry. I couldn't identify the exact source of my anger, but she poked and prodded me until I was able to get in touch with the feelings behind the anger. I was merely enduring my anger without defining the cause of it, and because I didn't allow myself to express my anger for the specific hurts and fears, the anger grew. I was like a heavy iron pot filled with boiling, steaming water, but with the lid sitting securely on top. By not loosening the lid to let the steam escape, it was ready to blow off, sky-high!

Standing in the Feelings

My counselor was forcing me to "stand in my feelings." When we're feeling uneasy, uncomfortable, or tempted, too often our first urge is to run to something that will (1) distract us from the feeling, (2) mask or help us avoid the feeling, or (3) provide some sort of substitute for what it is we're needing that we're not getting. By staying put for a moment, we can try to look beneath the feelings to the *cause* of the feelings. Ah-ha! And that's where we will begin to discover what's really going on inside. Emotions are a natural part of our lives. Being in touch with them and releasing them from time to time enables us to more appropriately manage them.

Being Honest about Our Feelings

When we're dealing with ongoing feelings that cause temptations, it is essential that we are first honest with ourselves and God and then with another person. Our feelings about men, or maybe our expectations of men, may lead us into ongoing thoughts, if not actions, that are not consistent with Christ's standard of purity. In *Boundaries*, authors Henry Cloud and

John Townsend describe it this way: "If I find that I have some pain or sin within, I need to open up and communicate it to God and others, so that I can be healed. Confessing pain and sin helps to 'get it out' so that it does not continue to poison me on the inside."[5] Scripture confirms this. A portion of James 5:16 reads: "Therefore, confess your sins to each other and pray for each other so that you may be healed."

In her book *The Cloister Walk*, Kathleen Norris explores in depth the lives and spiritual challenges of Benedictine sisters. One sister shares her story:

> The sister began to speak of her own life as a celibate woman. She had entered the convent in her late teens and a few years later, when she was still in formation—that is, she had not yet made lifelong vows as a Benedictine—she'd become infatuated with a priest. "I quickly learned," she said, "the truth of Psalm 32; I was miserable as long as I tried to keep it hidden. But as soon as I admitted to myself, and then to my novice mistress, what was going on, I felt an enormous release from guilt."[6]

Psalm 32 talks about the misery of unconfessed sin and the relief that comes from confession. Verses 4 and 5 read: "All day and all night your hand was heavy on me. My strength evaporated like water on a sunny day until I finally admitted all my sins to you and stopped trying to hide them. I said to myself, 'I will confess them to the LORD.' And you forgave me! All my guilt is gone" (TLB). Guilt is an interesting thing. We don't always recognize just how heavy it is until it's gone.

Get Real!

Recently our women's ministry pastor shared with me her frustration about how women in the church seem to feel a need to put on a "church face" around other women. Most of us do it. We may be miserable inside, but the moment our church shoes hit the church parking lot pavement, the "church face" goes on. We act the way we somehow believe "real Christian women" should act. We think we're supposed to be happy, holy, above reproach, and completely contented, so we act that way. But it's really fake. As a result, we tend to believe we are alone in our struggle to live joyful, godly lives. Believing that, we are tempted to hide our real, "unacceptable" selves all the more.

Being real with one another accomplishes two things: it exposes our sin to the light, and it encourages others to face and confess their sin as well.

What we're ignoring is God's grace. When Jesus died on the cross, it was so we could have a relationship with God *while we were still imperfect.* Romans 5:8 says, "But God demonstrates his own love for us in this: While we were still sinners, Christ died for us." As Christian sisters, we need to extend that same grace to one another. We need the freedom to be ourselves around one another. None of us is perfect.

What would happen if we could open up and pour out our feelings with just one other loving Christian woman? Would we discover that we are not alone? Believing we are alone in our sins and shortcomings is part of the great lie that keeps us chained to shame and guilt. Being real with one another accomplishes two things: it exposes our sin to the light, and it encourages others to face and confess their sin as well.

Confession and Accountability

Exposing our feelings and our temptations to the light takes the power out of them. It doesn't eliminate them, unfortunately. But it allows us to "vent," and it exposes the feelings for what they are.

It is important that we have genuine Christian friendships. Too often, even in the context of good relationships, the real us remains hidden. We need safe places to share our feelings, passions, and temptations. In *Hiding from Love*, Dr. John Townsend puts it this way: "It is not enough to simply be connected to others. We also need to bring out our hurt parts to those people, releasing them out of darkness and paralysis in the limbo of the isolation of the past."[7]

Safe People

As we begin to realize the importance of sharing our real selves, it's extremely important that we do so with safe people. The last thing we need is someone who will either react judgmentally or at the other extreme will minimize our weaknesses. We need people in our lives who will lovingly listen and encourage—and expect positive change and improvement from us.

Temptation and sin don't take holidays! We need partners in battle in order to win the war.

An "accountability buddy"—someone who will hold you accountable to overcoming temptation and sin in your life—is a real asset to your determination to grow and change. The key thing is to make your conversations *regular* and *real*. Temptation and sin don't take holidays! We need partners in battle in order to win the war.

Accountability to God

I love David. He is described as "a man after God's own heart" (1 Samuel 13:14). He wasn't afraid to pour out his feelings to God, whether songs of praise, cries of anguish, or rails of anger. He was real with his Lord. And I believe God honored him for that. God wants us to turn to him in times of trouble. He wants to be our Shoulder to cry on, our Friend to laugh with. He wants us to see that he is there for us in our most miserable of moments. And he wants us to share with him our innermost secrets and feelings.

He already knows everything about us. Hebrews 4:13 reads, "Nothing in all creation is hidden from God's sight. Everything is uncovered and laid bare before the eyes of him to whom we must give account." That should make it easy! Instead of trying to hide from him—which is impossible to do—we can pour out our hearts to him. We can ask him for strength to do the things we can't. We can let him hold us accountable. Like a dear friend, he'll be there to listen to our successes and triumphs as well as to our discouragements, failures, and confessions. Like a loving Daddy, he'll help us up, dust us off, bandage our skinned knees, and kiss our foreheads.

Psalm 139 is one of my favorites. Listen to just a few selected lines from the beginning of its rich text:

> You have examined my heart and know everything about me. . . . you know my every thought. You chart the path ahead of me. . . . You know what I am going to say before I even say it. You both precede me and follow me, and place your hand of blessing on my head. . . . I can *never* be lost to your Spirit! I can *never* get away from my God! . . . If I ride the morning winds to the farthest oceans, even there your hand will guide me, your strength will support me.
>
> verses 1–10 TLB

Now, this is a Dad who wants to be fully involved in our lives. Here's another verse that speaks to his desire to be intimately active in our spiritual growth: "I will instruct you (says the Lord) and guide you along the best pathway for your life; I will advise you and watch your progress" (Psalm 32:8 TLB). How's that for an accountability buddy?

My father-in-law spent some time driving a truck. His company installed regulators in each vehicle for the purpose of monitoring the speeds of its drivers. If a driver exceeded the freeway speed limit, the regulator would give off a warning beep.

We have God's Holy Spirit living in us. And if we are sensitive to his warning "beep," we, too, have a built in "regulator" to remind us when we are exceeding appropriate limits.

Listen to Your Heart

Feelings are important. It's healthy to not only recognize them but to also talk about them in safe places. Only then can you make conscious choices that will lead you along the road of abundant life.

When I was a little girl and was feeling frustrated, or angry, or confused about something, my mom encouraged me to sit down and write out a list of everything that was bothering me. The amazing thing was, it worked! And it still does. Somehow, seeing my emotions on paper gives them a sense of orderliness. Instead of vague, uncomfortable feelings, I am able to see them and sort them. I can "stand in them" to find underlying causes. I can check to see if there are old, untrue beliefs that are behind them. I can come up with God's truth about them. And even if I can't remedy the feelings, it seems to help just venting about them on paper.

With that in mind, I'd like to offer you a challenge. Take a moment to think about the thoughts and feelings that cause you to struggle. You will probably be tempted to put this off until later. But if you're like me, you may never get around to doing it if you don't do it now. If you don't want to write in the book, grab your journal. On the "Challenge!" worksheet that follows, you'll find examples to get you started. If they don't apply to you, simply cross them out. Be open and honest with yourself. Capture your true feelings and the temptations with which you struggle.

Chapter Summary

Step 3: Manage Your Feelings

1. Feelings are real, natural, and healthy.
2. You can choose to act on feelings, deny feelings, or acknowledge feelings and present them to God.
3. There are often deeper feelings beneath the feelings you are experiencing.
4. Confession and accountability are necessary for healing and growth.

Challenge!

Look over the following chart. A few examples are inserted to get you started. You can cross out all that do not apply to you.

- Start with the far left-hand column, "Feelings/Concerns." Work your way down by category and jot down anything and everything that comes to mind that's bothering you right now. Focus on one category at a time, then move to the next.
- Next, look at the far right-hand column, "Possible Solutions." Brainstorm any and all possible solutions. For now, don't worry about how realistic they are; you are simply coming up with as many potential solutions as you can.
- If you can, in the center column under "God's Truth," jot down any part of a Bible verse that comes to mind that seems to fit each situation or concern—and don't worry about references. For this task, some sort of Bible promises book (a little book that lists Scriptures by category) or a concordance will come in handy.

55

Feelings/Concerns	God's Truth	Possible Solutions
Spiritual		
• I keep messing up the same things	• He who has begun a good work in me . . . —*Phil. 1:6*	• Ask for forgiveness, then start again
Physical		
• I feel fat and ugly	• My body is his temple.— *Rom. 12:1*	• Know he loves me as *I am.* Ask him to help me with better food choices and discipline to exercise.
Emotional		
• I feel so alone	• He will never leave me nor forsake me —*Josh. 1:5*	• Feel his arms wrapped around me, loving me, supporting me. Tell him how I feel.
Relational		
• I'm angry with _____	• God forgives me; I need to forgive _____ —*Luke 6:37*	• I'll choose to forgive and decide how to lovingly discuss this hurt with _____. I'll also explore my anger.

Now, review the center and right columns. Think about the actions you can take to address your feelings and concerns, if you choose to do so. What are you willing to do this week?

_____

_____

_____

_____

Involve God in Your Resolve!

God is always a safe person to vent with. With him we can pour out our hearts, realizing that he already knows our deepest secrets and loves us anyway!

> *Abba, Daddy, I have so many feelings that I just don't know how to handle. My needs and desires are so real, and I sometimes feel so unfulfilled and empty. Remind me to bring these feelings to you! Teach me to "stand in my feelings" with you. Help me to get to the bottom of my "icebergs." Show me your truth about them. I know I can't do it alone, but that "I can do all things through Christ who strengthens me" (Philippians 4:13 NKJV). Lead me to other safe women who will hold me accountable. Give us the courage to be real with one another. Teach us to listen lovingly and to confront honestly. And Father, I praise you because you are patient with your children (2 Peter 3:9). Thank you for loving me!*

What else do you want to ask God right now? What else do you want to tell him?

_____

_____

_____

_____

_____

I pray this in the name of your precious Son, Jesus. Amen.

What do you sense he is saying to you right now?

_____

_____

_____

_____

Recognize Common Traps

Thou hast made us for thyself, O God,
And the heart of man is restless
until it finds its rest in thee.

St. Augustine

Have you ever had a chocolate kind of day? You know what I mean—you just can't get through the day without it. It's all you can think about. You *must* have it. No, you *need* it! Or am I the only one?

We now have some welcome scientific evidence to support our genuine *need* for chocolate—well, the dark kind anyway. We can take comfort in the knowledge that there are true health benefits—reduction in blood pressure, improved circulation, lower cholesterol. Best of all, it contains "happy juice." The real name is *anandamide*, which is a neurotransmitter, but "happy juice" sort of says it all. So that's why we reach for the chocolate when we're feeling low or stressed out. We eat it and we feel better. But besides making us feel good, what does chocolate—or any comfort food for that matter—do for us? A couple of things. It temporarily takes our focus off what we're feeling, and it provides temporary pleasure.

When we experience feelings that relate to unmet needs and expectations, it's quite common for us to look for something that will quickly "fix" the problem. However, choosing something that simply provides temporary relief won't solve the problem of the unmet need. *As long as we ignore the real need, the uncomfortable feelings will keep coming back.* And if we choose inappropriate ways to satisfy our needs, we will ultimately miss out on God's best for our lives.

Our need to placate ourselves often indicates that something is out of whack in our emotions or our lives. As we begin to understand and recognize the behaviors we fall into, they can serve as "red flags" that will alert us to pay attention to our feelings.

As long as we ignore the real need, the uncomfortable feelings will keep coming back.

When I feel an overwhelming need to munch on chocolate, that's usually a clear signal for me that I'm feeling stressed or uncomfortable about something. That also tells me it's time to stop for a moment and figure out what's going on. So instead of automatically reaching for the Snickers bar, I can spend a moment or two figuring out what it is that's bothering me. When I enlist God's aid, he will help. Once I can get to the root of what's bothering me, I'm better able to deal with it in a healthy and productive way. Until I do that, the feelings and the urges for things that distract or mask my discomfort just keep revisiting me.

As we work through the rest of this chapter, I'd like to challenge you to think about the things you sometimes do in order to feel good, or to avoid feeling bad.

How We Cope

Let's talk about some of the traps we fall into when that empty, needy spot begins to squirm. You won't find these terms in any Psych 101 textbook. I know; I've looked. But they make much more sense to me than the sophisticated labels. And for the purpose of discussion, I've arbitrarily arranged these behavioral tactics into three general categories. When we're feeling "less than," it's easy to run to any one of these feeling-altering behaviors.

1. Chasing Shiny Objects—Tuning Out *with* Distractions

Do you remember the character Dory in the Disney movie *Finding Nemo*? She was the bright blue fish with the short memory and shorter attention span. To get her distracted, Marlin simply pointed and said, "Look, Dory! Shiny object!" whereupon Dory excitedly took off in the direction indicated.

We can be like that. When feelings grow uncomfortable, it's much easier to distract ourselves than to feel what we're feeling, let alone stop to examine what's causing the feelings. And it's so easy to do. Distractions come in all kinds of pretty packages. And most often, there is nothing inherently wrong with them.

There's the distraction of TV, now available on hundreds of channels, 24/7. Shopping is great fun and can keep the mind engaged for hours on end. One of my favorite distractions is email. No matter what else I'm doing, I love seeing the little icon show up in the lower right-hand corner of my screen announcing that I have mail.

Let's see, what else can distract us? How about computer solitaire? Or video games, Internet browsing, endless techie toys, music, movies, even a good book.

If those activities aren't enough to pack our day so full and keep us so distracted that we don't really have to think about feelings, we often resort to doing things "better." Hobbies become obsessive. Work hours grow longer and longer. Perfectionism—just how clean does a house or car need to be? Never-ending projects. Organizing to the extreme. When things are done to excess, it may be time to stop and ask yourself, "*Why* am I doing this? What's this *really* about? What am I running *away* from?"

Busyness is a sophisticated method of distraction and can even be a means of escape. If I don't slow down, I won't have to look my feelings in the eye. Remember my counselor's advice to "stand in the pain"? It's hard—and often uncomfortable—to do. It's much easier to keep moving, to keep busy. If we stop, we might begin to feel. And if we feel, we might begin to hurt. And if we hurt, we might have to deal with it. And dealing with it is difficult. It's easier to just keep going, going, going and not feel the discomfort at all. The problem is, discomfort and pain are the ways our bodies and minds communicate with us. If we're not listening, the problem will only grow bigger and deeper. More important, when we refuse to face our pain and grow through it, we're missing out. We'll continue to fill our lives with the unimportant instead of with the amazing.

I heard an acronym for the word *busy* a few years ago, and it's really appropriate:

> Being
> Under
> Satan's
> Yoke.

Pretty good, huh? God didn't intend for our lives to be filled to the brim with "doings." He desires us to sometimes simply "be." When we're busy, it's hard to hear his still small voice. And it's his voice that will lead us into perfect contentment.

2. Numbing Out—Turning Off *with Escape*

"Escaping" is when we block out discomfort by escaping from or numbing our feelings. You've probably seen someone jokingly cover her ears and loudly repeat, "La-La-La-La!" indicating she doesn't want to hear what you're saying. That's pretty much what this is—choosing to "shut down" so we don't have to feel what we're feeling.

We may be in denial because sometimes reality seems too hard to bear. We may just feel a need to "check out" for a while—completely avoid thinking or feeling anything for a time. We may stuff our feelings deep down and try to convince ourselves that they're gone—*poof,* vanished!

For many of us, turning off is easier than running away, especially if that has worked for us in the past. But there is a price to pay for emotional shutdown—in relationships as well as in our own emotional health.

Typical blocking behaviors can include activities generally considered normal except that, to numb and anesthetize our pain and discomfort, they are taken to the extreme. Whereas *tuning out* serves to provide a temporary distraction, *turning off* begins to border on self-destructive behavior.

Gwen felt overwhelmed with the stresses of life, so sleep was an escape. She didn't have to think about all the things that upset her when she was zonked on her pillow. The trouble was, when she woke up, the problems were still there. A nap is an okay thing, but when you find yourself constantly seeking sleep as a means of escape from your reality, that's a red flag, especially when it is interfering with your ability to function normally on a day-to-day basis. When friends confronted Gwen honestly with their concerns about her, that was her wake-up call.

Patsy loves mystery novels. But when she's feeling extreme emotional pressure, it's easy for her to fall into the trap of excessive reading. Being immersed in the drama of the story is much more fun than facing the reality of her own life. Patsy realized her recreational reading had become a "numb-out" problem when she noticed herself having unusual reactions to her reading. Whenever she finished a book, she felt an almost desperate need to begin a new one. So she would go buy more. And more. As soon as she finished one book, she would obsessively dive into another. She preferred her books to time with her friends and other activities. But the kicker for Patsy was when the characters in her books began to seem almost real to her. Needless to say, she realized that was not normal, so she began to work at unraveling the mystery behind her emotional escapes in reading.

Jan "turned off" by isolating herself. It began gradually. She declined more and more social invitations. She rationalized not going to church every week. She dreaded the beginning of the workweek and called in sick almost every other Monday. In time, she found it difficult to leave the house just to pick up groceries. Her house was her haven, her safe place. A place where she didn't need to face the world. She numbed it all out. Until she was able to face her emotions and deal with them, she was a prisoner in her own home.

These are only a few examples of how we use escapism to avoid feelings, but the list is endless. Regardless of the symptoms, it is important to remember that the root cause is the same: pain and discomfort from unmet needs. If there are more serious or life-threatening behaviors involved, such as alcohol and substance abuse, it is important that you seek the qualified help of a pastor or Christian counselor. A good counselor will help you gain insight into the Word of God as you explore the reasons behind your difficulty. In order to grow, we all need to be willing to face our pain and allow God to heal us.

3. Cozying in the Comfort Quilt—Turning On with Substitutions

When we're not feeling what we *want* to feel, we may try to *manufacture* the feelings. Just as snuggling in a big, fluffy comforter can make us feel warm and cozy, we may resort to substitutions that make us feel that way. It may seem as innocuous as a romance novel, a favorite soap opera, or a somewhat racy movie. But it is altering our state of feeling into more of what we want to feel.

Substitutions become more serious when women turn to things that are potentially harmful, such as office flirtations, pornography, promiscuity, or affairs.

Anita seemed to have it all together. But inside, she was hurting. She had expected more from her husband, but he never seemed to appreciate her for who she was. At home she often felt ignored, passed by. Work was a different story. There she was respected for her excellent work and well liked for her energy and sense of humor.

One co-worker in particular seemed to enjoy playful conversation with her. When one day it veered toward subtle innuendo, her head told her she should draw the line, but her heart resonated with those warm feelings of being the object of attraction. She rationalized, "It can't hurt. I'm not doing anything wrong. It will never go anywhere." And so she responded with mild flirtation. She and her co-worker ended up having an affair. Oh, she never intended for it to happen. But one small compromise at a time led her down a path of difficult return. Her heart won over her head, and she fell into the big trap.

We need to protect our minds and hearts against anything that would lead us astray.

Did you know that more than half of all office affairs begin with a *simple friendship?* God's Word tells us, "Above all else, guard your affections" (Prov. 4:23 TLB), and there is a reason for that. We are emotionally wired creatures. We need to protect our minds and hearts against anything that would lead us astray.

Secret Traps

Women love to talk, but there are a whole lot of things that we as women *don't* talk about. Some of those things have to do with the yearnings we feel—to be cherished and adored by someone. To be pursued with passion. We also don't talk about the things we think and do behind closed doors in an effort to experience those wonderful feelings.

- Some women turn to fantasy—creating elaborate romantic scenarios in their minds about real or imagined men.
- Some cross the line in what they read or watch in movies.
- It's easy to rationalize reasons to touch or hug a man in order to connect with him. And it's easy to make it look innocent and socially acceptable.
- More and more women are getting caught up in pornography.
- Single women may be promiscuous; married women may have affairs.

The list goes on and on.

Opening the Door

When we choose to dwell on thoughts that are less than pure, we are opening the door to further disobedience and sinful behaviors. It's fairly easy to rationalize almost any small indiscretion. The problem is, one small indiscretion can easily lead to another. And another. This includes indiscretions in the mind as well. When we use our imaginations to create a fantasy situation, we are paving the way for our actions to follow. In James 1:14–15 we read, "But each one is tempted when, by [her] own evil desire, [she] is dragged away and enticed. Then, after desire has conceived, it gives birth to sin; and sin, when it is full-grown, gives birth to death." The story of my battle with The Beast perfectly demonstrates this very truth. What began as fantasy eventually grew into a full-blown addiction.

Fantasy

Discussing the serious impact of romantic fantasy on women, Mari Hanes says, "Counselors and analysts tell us that a woman's most constant romantic fantasies and daydreams are often indications of her inner needs. It is obvious, however, to both Christian and secular counselors that even though fantasy may indicate inner emotional needs, fantasy alone cannot meet those needs."[1] In fact, only God can fulfill our needs.

Imagination is a wonderful, God-given thing. But Hanes goes on to say, "Yet, if the strength of the imagination is that it can enhance reality, the danger is that it can be used to avoid unpleasant reality. In this way, one's dream world can steal away the joy of the real world."[2] We rob ourselves of joy!

That's exactly what happened to me. Because I was so completely focused on the fantasy of the moment for such a long time, I missed out on years of my life.

I remember being out for a really wonderful evening with friends. We had dinner downtown, then headed for the theater to see *42nd Street*—a terrific musical. But somewhere in the middle of it, I slipped into my fantasy world. I remember consciously thinking, "What am I doing! I'll never see this play again!" Unfortunately, the pull was too strong. I ended up lost in my own head for the duration of the play and missed out on the experience.

During those addictive years, so much of what was real and wonderful and right there in front of me just couldn't compete with my fantasies.

Real men can't compete either. If you're married and fantasizing about another man—or even a fictitious man—your husband will never measure up. He can't. He's real and he's human.

And if you're single and caught up in a fantasy about your dream guy, you might as well give up right now. He doesn't exist in the real world.

Infatuation

Falling into infatuation is a common thing for women. But there are obvious pitfalls. We easily become obsessive, and that takes our focus off God as well as the day-to-day joy in our lives. The crucial thing to consider about infatuation is that we tend to look at the invented person rather than the real one. We see only Prince Charming on his white horse, not the dirty leggings thrown on the floor in the castle bathroom.

We see only Prince Charming on his white horse, not the dirty leggings thrown on the floor in the castle bathroom.

A friend of mine asked to talk with me. It turned out Sarah was thinking about divorcing her husband and wanted my advice about the "dating world." I had met her husband at a previous office function. He was very attractive and seemed rather nice as well. They had been married for seven years, so I asked her a number of questions about their relationship. Here's a shortened version of our conversation:

"Well, Sarah, does he treat you badly?"

"No, not at all. In fact, he's very attentive, remembers special occasions, and once in a while brings me flowers for no specific reason."

"Has he ever been unfaithful?"

"Heavens, no! He's actually really crazy about me."

"You both work outside the home. Does he help out around the house?"

"Yes. He's great about pitching in with whatever needs doing. And he's a good cook too."

"Well, do the two of you get along okay? I mean, do you fight or argue?"

"No. He's easy to be around, and we do have a lot of fun together."

By now I was a bit confused as to the problem, so I just came out and asked, "So, what's the problem? He sounds incredible! Why are you thinking of getting a divorce?" And I will never forget how stunned I was with her answer.

"Well, it's just that he's really the only guy I ever dated. There's this guy at work I'm attracted to, and I think about him all the time. I would love to be able to date. I'm afraid I might be missing out on something out there."

Here was an intelligent woman about to throw away her marriage to an exceptional man just to experience the "thrill of the dating life" as she perceived it in her mind! I can hear the resounding laughter of 95 percent of you single women out there reading this right now. Don't worry. I set her straight.

Romance Novels and Soaps

If this hits a hot button, I'd like to ask you to keep an open mind. I'm offering an opinion, but personal decisions are always between us and the Lord.

Novels and soaps that focus on romance and passion claim to be filling a need. But are they really? The warm, exciting feelings are nice, but they are temporary and typically leave us dissatisfied once the pleasure wears off. And, like any other substitute, they can lead to addiction.

Here's one woman's experience with romance novels:

There was a time when I couldn't put them down. I had a tendency to shut out my family and ignore my responsibilities.

I read this material for years before, and after, becoming a Christian. It caused problems in my relationships and my marriage. My husband hauled the novels out of our home by the boxful.

I thought I was the only person with this problem. But recently I have found others, and it is causing problems for them too. [People should be warned] of these books and the potential damage they can do.[3]

It doesn't need to be an addiction to be damaging. Whenever we allow a substitute to fill a real need in our lives, it's important to stop and take a closer look. When in doubt, we should pray about it. We can ask God to evaluate what we bring into our lives.

The Internet

Most of us are aware of the multitude of dangers on the Internet, and we know enough to stay away from the obviously bad things. But much like dabbling with fantasy, it's easy to rationalize brief explorations into sites that pique our curiosity. Sadly, although pornography used to be almost exclusively the domain of men, more and more young girls and women are getting pulled into this disturbing addiction.

Less obvious, in terms of inherent danger, are chat rooms. They seem harmless enough and can certainly be just that—harmless. Informative, even. But an interesting phenomenon is taking place. Because of the anonymity we can have in cyberspace, people seem to feel more freedom to stray from their moral and ethical values. Who's to know? There is also safety in knowing we can simply cease to participate at any given time.

Like with so many other temptations, chat rooms make it easy to step outside our boundaries. We can strike up conversations and develop friendships with people we may never actually meet. And we may talk about things we would never think of talking about with someone in person. One woman says, "It started innocently—but before I knew it, my online relationship consumed my life. . . . He persisted, saying, 'Are you Christians afraid to talk about such things?' I soon found myself . . . revealing things about myself I would never talk about with a man face-to-face. A different kind of intimacy developed. . . . It felt like a game. It was easy to forget there was a real person at the other end. My game quickly became an addiction."[4]

Self-Gratification

Because the question comes up so frequently, we're going to very briefly discuss masturbation. Does the Bible address this specific issue? Not directly, but let's be honest with ourselves. Shannon Ethridge, in her book *Every Woman's Battle*, doesn't mince words on this subject: "When women masturbate, they don't think pure thoughts, and the Bible is very clear about that issue (see Philippians 4:8). We don't entertain thoughts that are pure, noble, or praiseworthy when we engage in self-gratification. Women who masturbate have some fantasy about another person, some scenario, some ritual they play out in their minds in order to reach orgasm. These thoughts are a stench to God."[5] In his book *Addicted to Love*, Steve Arterburn talks about the self-destructive side of self-gratification when he says, "Compulsive masturbation, built on fantasy (and/or) pornography, is an escape from intimacy."[6] Instead it becomes a selfish act that only *fuels* our sexual desires, rather than satisfying them.

Quench the Thirst!

Mari Hanes paints a clear picture of our choice between two cups:

> A woman's emotional and sexual needs can create a great thirst. We each have two cups set before us from which we can drink. One is the chalice filled with undisciplined fantasies and unchecked actions. From the outside, it appears beautiful and desirable. But before your thirst pushes you to lift the chalice and drink, look closely into the contents. Mixed into this drink are seeds of destruction, spiritual parasites, the contamination of what the Bible calls "a cup of demons."
>
> The other exquisite chalice is filled with "the best wine," pure and costly like the miracle wine Jesus provided for the wedding feast in Cana of Galilee.[7]

The "cup of demons" remark might seem a bit strong, but perhaps it causes us to stop and think. What are we "drinking"? What are we pouring into our minds and hearts? Is it the "pure and costly" love of Christ? Or is it a poor and temporary substitute that the world offers? Only God can quench our thirst; anything else only increases the cravings and the dissatisfaction. This is described in Ephesians 4:19: "Having lost all sensitivity, they have given themselves over to sensuality so as to indulge in every kind of impurity, with a *continual lust for more*" (emphasis mine). Paul then goes on to say, "Put off your old self, which is being corrupted by its deceitful desires; to be made new in the attitude of your minds; and to put on the new self, created to be like God in true righteousness and holiness" (Ephesians 4:22–24).

Only God can quench our thirst; anything else only increases the cravings and the dissatisfaction.

Recognizing the Traps

So, what are your traps? What things tempt you to feel the way you want to feel? What kinds of substitutes are easy for you to rationalize as okay? I was in some strange way able to rationalize thoughts and behaviors that I now see as absolutely horrid and unthinkable. My prayer is that you won't make the same mistake. Recognizing and understanding your traps gives you the "ah-ha!" you need in order to stop and think about what's really going on. Then you can take your discomfort and thirst to the Lord. He will fill your cup until it runs over!

Chapter Summary

Step 4: Recognize Common Traps

1. Avoidance, distractions, and substitutions are common traps.
2. It's important that you recognize the traps that tempt you so you can deal with them effectively.
3. Traps often look good—sometimes even harmless—on the outside, but they keep you from God's best for your life.
4. Traps may provide temporary comfort, but only God can give you lasting joy.

Challenge!

1. Think about some of the ways you cope with your need to feel loved and valued.
   a. Do you recognize any "distraction" (tuning out) behaviors?

   _____

   _____

   _____

   b. "Escape" (turning off) behaviors?

   _____

   _____

   _____

c. "Substitution" (turning on) behaviors?

_____

_____

_____

2. Try to "stand in your feelings" for a moment. When you cope in the above ways, what are the feelings and unmet needs *underneath* the behaviors? Ask God to reveal what he wants you to see.

_____

_____

_____

_____

3. What is one coping behavior you want to change right now? Why?

_____

_____

_____

_____

4. Describe the benefits of making this change.

_____

_____

_____

_____

Involve God in Your Resolve!

Ask him to show you where you may be missing out on his best for you. Look to him to meet your every need.

Dearest Father, you understand my greatest needs and desires. In my attempts to get those needs met, I don't always do the right or best things. Open my mind to begin exploring behaviors that are getting in the way of true happiness. If I'm rationalizing about anything, open my eyes to see what it is. "Search me, O God, and know my heart. . . . See if there is any offensive way in me" (Psalm 139:23–24). Give me the courage to decline what the world offers with all its temptations. I want to drink from your "exquisite chalice," filled with your best and most costly wine. Help me to believe your truth and to see myself as I am—your princess. Teach me how to act, think, and feel like the daughter of the almighty King!

What else do you want to ask God right now? What else do you want to tell him?

_____

_____

_____

_____

_____

I pray this in the name of your precious Son, Jesus. Amen.

What do you sense he is saying to you right now?

_____

_____

_____

_____

Part II

Our Reality

Step 5

Accept God's Standards

Purity is something far too deep for me to arrive at naturally. But when the Holy Spirit comes into me, He brings into the center of my personal life the very Spirit that was exhibited in the life of Jesus Christ, namely, the Holy Spirit, which is absolute unblemished purity.

Oswald Chambers

In the past four chapters we talked about our many unmet needs, the genuine feelings that often demand our attention because of those needs, and the traps into which we sometimes fall, either in an effort to avoid discomfort or to create the feelings we so deeply want to feel.

God gives us guidelines for complete fulfillment. For joy beyond our expectations. For love that defies description. For feelings of worth and value that transcend our imaginations.

But he gives us some of these "guidelines" as *commandments* for a reason. First, they're really nonnegotiable from his perspective. Second, we may not take them seriously if we feel they are only suggestions. Third, they are intended to groom us to be the very individuals God designed us to be—humble, repentant, obedient, holy, and destined for heaven.

Although many of his lessons are given to us in the form of parables, letters, personal accounts, and observations, they too are part of the Word we are commanded to obey. "This is love for God: to obey his commands" (1 John 5:3).

When we hold up his firm expectations against the morality of our present culture, they seem tight and restrictive. So we sometimes stiffen and rebel and determine to do things our own way. But what we may see as rules and restrictions are actually the deep wisdom of a loving parent. A perfect Father, in fact.

Anything he asks of us is for our best good.

Think about it. A mother constantly directs a child: "Don't touch that oven door—it's hot!" "Stop! There's a car coming!" Is she doing that to be hard or mean? No. She's protecting her child. She wants her son to avoid a bad burn. She prevents her daughter from being hit by a car.

God does the same thing with us as his adored children. "Don't covet! It will fill you with discontent." "Forgive that person who hurt you so badly. If you don't, the anger will eat you up inside."

Have you ever watched a little three-year-old so exhausted she is in hyperdrive? What is likely to happen when her daddy tells her it's time to take a nap? She kicks and screams. She doesn't want to go. Yet the dad knows what's best for her. And after her nap she is a happier, more contented child.

God is like that father. He knows us better than we know ourselves. He is the Master Designer, so he knows what makes each of us tick. "For you created my inmost being; you knit me together in my mother's womb" (Psalm 139:13). He has watched us from our birth and knows everything we've been through. And the Master Designer has a Master Plan, as well. "'For I know the plans I have for you,' declares the LORD, 'plans to prosper you and not to harm you, plans to give you hope and a future'" (Jeremiah 29:11).

Anything he asks of us is for our *best* good. When we try to do it on our own, we get battered by the world. When we stick with him and his Word, it's much easier. "And his commands are not burdensome, for everyone born of God overcomes the world" (1 John 5:3–4). He gives us his laws because he knows that's the only way we'll ever be *truly* happy. Happy in spite of our outward circumstances.

The Parable of All of Us

You may know the story. A man had two sons, and one day the younger one came to him and asked for his share of the estate so he could go off and live life as he pleased (see Luke 15:11–32). What you may not know is that within the culture at that time, his demand demonstrated an "arrogant disregard for his father's authority as head of the family."[1] He then went off and "squandered his wealth in wild living" (v. 13). That's exactly what I did. I disregarded my loving, compassionate Father—and his authority—and proceeded to squander my life.

In the parable, the son hit on hard times. He was finally reduced to the repulsive and degrading task of feeding pigs. And he was so hungry that he wished he could eat what they were eating. Especially considering that Jews avoided even touching pigs because they were considered defiled, the young man sank to a new low, indeed.

Finally, he returned home, humiliated and hungry. He hoped his father was willing to take him back—as a servant, not as a son. He recognized that his father's servants had a far better life than he did. As he sheepishly approached home, he found his father waiting for him, running toward him with open arms. What joy was experienced in the reunion!

Like the prodigal, we too can come running back to the Father, finding welcome in his arms and love in his eyes.

In Hindsight

I saw God's way as narrow and restrictive, rather than a way of discipline that would lead to lasting comfort and genuine love. His love was right there in front of me all the time. But he is a gentleman. He patiently waits for each of us to figure things out and learn from our mistakes. He gives us *choice*. Isn't it remarkable that the word *choice* means the ability to choose for ourselves, and it also means "the best"? He is the *choice* choice!

Compromise

I firmly believe that the greatest threat to the church to-day—to the body of Christ itself—is the gradual compromise in the standards of his people.

You've probably heard the story about the frog in hot water. It depicts a frightening truth for us. Imagine what happens if we drop a frog into a pot of hot water—he immediately senses the heat and leaps out of the pot before he is hurt. However, if you put that same frog into a pot of cold water, turn the heat on, and let the water temperature rise gradually, he adapts to the increasing temperature and, rather than sensing the danger, will boil to death. Scary thought, huh?

You can see where I'm going with this.

This is only my observation, but it seems to me that often we as Christians focus on keeping a comfortable gap between ourselves and what the rest of the world is doing. That way we can look at people in "the world" and feel confident and smug that we are not nearly as bad as they are. But the world with its culture is going downhill. And as it gradually slides down into the dark abyss, we are staying just an appropriate level above it and apart from it, but we are nevertheless sliding in right behind it.

Think for just a moment about the images we see on TV and the lyrics we hear in music. Compare the content with just ten years ago. Or twenty. The decline in moral standards is astounding. Yet most of us continue to watch and listen.

Often we are content to be not quite as bad as the world.

Instead of comparing ourselves to God's purity and striving to do everything possible to narrow the gap between *him* and *us*, often we are content to be not quite as bad as the world. In *I Saw the Lord*, Anne Graham Lotz states, "Under ordinary lighting, as we set our own standards, compare ourselves with others, do what feels good and what we think is right in our own eyes, we can be deluded into thinking we're okay. In fact, we can even think we are better than others, confident that God must be pleased with us."[2]

God's Best

Bottom line, he wants his best for us. *Big picture* best. Not today best. Not this month or this year best. *Eternity* best.

So with that in mind, let's explore his Word and reexamine his "perfect law that gives freedom" (James 1:25) in light of the fact he truly wants us to feel deeply loved, cherished, adored, and valued.

God's Standard for Purity

In his well-known Christian classic *My Utmost for His Highest*, Oswald Chambers says this about purity: "God has only one intended destiny for mankind—holiness. . . . Holiness means *absolute purity* of your walk before God, the words coming from your mouth, and every thought in your minds—placing every detail of your life under the scrutiny of God Himself" (emphasis mine).[3]

Wow. Absolute purity. That's a tall order.

What things have I been thinking about today? Have all my thoughts been pure? What about my reading material, my choices on TV? Where have they been leading my mind? God doesn't beat around the bush when it comes to his standards. Let's look further at what he says in 1 Peter 1:15–16: "But be holy now in everything you do, just as the Lord is holy, who invited you to be his child. He himself has said, 'You must be holy, for I am holy'" (TLB).

The word "holy" occurs several times in this passage, so what exactly does that mean? The NIV Life Application Study Bible states it this way: "Holiness means being totally devoted or dedicated to God, set apart and different, not blending in with the crowd. . . . Our focus and priorities must be his."[4]

Again, I need to ask myself some questions. How am I different? Are his qualities showing up in my life? When I'm feeling "needy," is my focus on him and his Word? Am I more interested in his priorities than my own emotional feelings?

Here's another challenging comment. In The Practice of Godliness, Jerry Bridges writes:

> John said he wrote his first letter so that his readers would not sin (1 John 2:1). Most Christians seem content not to sin very much, but John's goal was that we not sin at all. Every sin, no matter how small it may seem to us, is an affront to God's authority, a disregard for His law, a spurning of His love. Because of this, sin cannot be tolerated in any form, to any degree. That "inconsequential" lie, that "just a little bit" of dishonesty, that fleeting lustful look, offends our holy God and wages war against our own souls (1 Peter 2:11).[5]

Wow. This one pulls me up short. I know I miss the mark in many ways. Am I content with that? Do I rationalize? Do I find myself saying, "Just this once" about things I want to do or see or think about, instead of laying my desires before the Lord? Am I overlooking or ignoring the small sins in my life?

What is "sin," anyway? Is it an official list of "don'ts" or a collection of offenses mentioned in the Bible? Certainly God makes many sins plain in his Word. But what about the things that are not specifically addressed in the Bible? For example, we won't find anything that talks about romance novels, will we? Or drugs. Or pornography.

What about the gray areas? For example, behavior on a date, what we watch on TV or what we read, interactions with men who are not our husbands, Internet chat room relationships. Where do we draw the line between what's okay for us and what's not healthy? What is sinful and what is not?

The bottom-line question for the committed Christian is, How will this influence my thought life and my walk with God?

I personally like the definition of sin provided by Cynthia Heald in her book *Becoming a Woman of Excellence*: "Sin—Whatever weakens your reason, impairs the tenderness of your conscience, obscures your sense of God, or takes off the relish of spiritual things, that thing is sin for you, however innocent it may be in itself."[6] This makes it personal. It begins by assuming I'm keeping my heart tender toward God. If I shut him out, I won't even be aware of my sense of him. This definition also holds me to a very high standard. It's not about where I draw the line with what I can and cannot do; it insists that I'm looking to him to show me what's best for me.

Because he loves me.

We have to practice good judgment and discernment. The bottom-line question for the committed Christian is, How will this influence my thought life and my walk with God? If we earnestly seek him, and if we're willing to delve into the Word and honestly look for God's intentions, we'll find answers to our questions.

His Strength, Not Mine

Let's stop here for a moment. We've just looked at some pretty high expectations, and that can feel daunting.

No matter how hard we try, we cannot walk in purity without his strength. He admonishes us to "be strong in the Lord and in his mighty power" (Ephesians 6:10). He also says to us, "So do not fear, for I am with you; do not be dismayed, for I am your God. I will strengthen you and help you; I will uphold you with my righteous right hand" (Isaiah 41:10). It helps to fill our minds with these promises, and then take him at his Word. We must *lean* on him—put all our hope for victory in his hands.

Purity is one area where we should NOT set "realistic expectations" for ourselves; *we need to expect from ourselves what God expects*, and we cannot accomplish those expectations without his supernatural power. We can't be determined enough, tough enough, or committed enough to do it on our own. He tells us, "My grace is sufficient for you, for my power is made perfect in [your] weakness" (2 Corinthians 12:9). Jesus was fully God and fully man, and in his humanness on earth he encountered everything we experience today. He understands. He also knows we are *only* human; it's not a matter of if we will fail, because we will fail. But he sees our hearts.

We need to expect from ourselves what God expects, and we cannot accomplish those expectations without his supernatural power.

His Word demonstrates that he is gentle with those who have hearts for him. Speaking about God's grace toward the many godly men in the Old Testament who stumbled, A. W. Tozer tells us in his classic *The Pursuit of God* that "the man of God set his heart to exalt God above all; God accepted his *intention* as fact and acted accordingly. *Not perfection, but holy intention made the difference*" (emphasis mine).[7]

86

Our job is to set our hearts and our wills for him and to then trust him to be our strength because we know that "the Spirit helps us in our weakness" (Romans 8:26).

The Questions Begin

The Bible is pretty clear about God's standard of holiness and his intolerance of sin. The big question for me for some time now has been, Are some things that may be wrong for one person okay for someone else?

Here's an example. When I was a volunteer with our church high school group, one of the girls shared a problem with me. It seems that Abby's parents were very conscientious about not bringing home videos with foul language. They were trying to protect Abby. However, the romantic and somewhat sexual content was occasionally borderline. That made Abby very uncomfortable. I knew her parents to be good people and encouraged her to discuss her feelings with them.

They were surprised, to say the least. They were trying to protect her from what was hard on their ears, never guessing that the semi-sensual parts—completely comfortable for them—were causing Abby to struggle.

So there you have it. Opposite sensitivities.

Is it simply an *individual* issue? Or are we ALL called to the *highest* of moral standards? God instructs us to think about what is true, noble, right, pure, lovely, admirable, excellent, and praiseworthy (Philippians 4:8). So when we fill our minds with words, thoughts, and images that are lascivious and immoral, are we catering to our "lower nature"? Are we poisoning our thought life? At best, we are desensitizing ourselves to what *should* offend us. At worst, we are allowing some pretty horrid "videotapes" to be downloaded into our minds.

God has made it clear to me, because of my past woundedness, that I need to steer clear of some very specific things in order to stay healthy. And I definitely feel convicted at those times when I approach those boundaries, so I now avoid those things. But I allow myself to *rationalize* reading and watching other things that include bad language, sexual innuendo, and moderate violence. "If it gets too bad," I tell myself, "I'll turn off the TV or put down the book." But even if I do, does that make it okay to start watching it or reading it in the first place?

The World's Perspective

Almost everything we see today on TV and in movies depicts blatant sexual immorality as perfectly normal and socially acceptable. Much of it is couched in comedy to make it more easily and comfortably digested. Laughter obscures the discomfort we *should* be feeling. Satan is no dummy—he's a cunning adversary.

Mary Ellen Ashcroft, in her candid book *Temptations Women Face*, writes,

> We cooperate with the world's temptation to linger by seeing movies or reading novels that promote unhealthy sexual activity and make fidelity or abstinence more difficult. The world would like us all to remain in this breathless, selfish stage of sexuality; it would like all of us to stick at the maturity level [of a turned-on thirteen-year-old]. . . . Because the world, the flesh and the devil delight (as usual) to distort a good gift from God . . . they twist it to offer us temptations . . . [even though] we know the temptation to remain in an adolescent sexuality . . . is self-consumed and never satisfied.[8]

Again, exposing ourselves to things that titillate and feed our desires only creates more aching hunger.

Again, exposing ourselves to things that titillate and feed our desires only *creates more aching hunger.*

We also need to consider that TV programs, books, and other entertainment venues can be *addictive* as well. We talked about the process of addiction in chapter 4. To me that means we regularly need to honestly evaluate our reading and viewing habits by asking ourselves a few questions:

1. Am I becoming "hooked" on this? Am I becoming a slave to it?
2. What exactly is it about the show/book/whatever that is so enticing? Is it something I should avoid?
3. What "pure and lovely things" am I missing out on while I'm spending time with this activity?
4. If I *objectively examine* this from a spiritual perspective—and perhaps compare it with Philippians 4:8—exactly what am I feeding into my mind on a regular basis—am I *feasting* on impure material that God surely finds offensive?
5. Am I willing to lay this before the Lord?

Lord, I lift this up to you. I trust you for your insight, wisdom, and guidance. Reveal to me how you see it. And help me choose to be obedient.

Lack of Reality

In addition to the issues of morality, self-focus, and desensitization, there is something else about how sexuality and relationships are portrayed in the media that endangers our minds: lack of reality. Bodies are hard and sleek, relationships are intense, outcomes are exciting. How does that make us feel about ourselves and our lives? If we flood our minds with "pretend" reality, suddenly we begin to feel we're missing something. And here come those nagging sentiments—"I'm not attractive enough, my husband isn't romantic enough, and my life is boring!" Once again, we are drawn into the temptation to find our own solutions to feel better or to feel nothing at all. Our need becomes our focus.

If we can agree that what we focus on determines outcome—and I believe we can all agree this is substantiated enough both scripturally and psychologically—then perhaps those of us who need to should ask ourselves why we are allowing ourselves to ingest so much questionable material. Especially in light of God's standards. Once we get our eyes back on Jesus and his high expectations, the things of the world begin to look pretty dingy by comparison!

The *Journey* toward Holiness

How I wish for pixie dust, the kind of magical powder Tinkerbell used to make dreams come true in *Peter Pan*. With it, we could be transformed in a snap. But God has charted our paths and knows exactly what we need to learn and when. It is in this journey toward heaven that God hones and refines our character and our person. The destination is sure; the journey has much to do with our willingness to cooperate with God.

Father truly does know best!

And as we choose to turn our backs on impurity to embrace holiness, we will discover the pure happiness, satisfaction, and fulfillment only he can give. We will discover that Father *truly does* know best!

Chapter Summary

Step 5: Accept God's Standards

1. God's laws are not just nonnegotiable commandments but a blueprint for true happiness and fulfillment.
2. As the Master Designer, he knows you better than you know yourself.
3. Keep your focus on narrowing the gap between your standards and God's perfection, rather than being satisfied that your behaviors are better than those of the world.
4. God's standard is absolute purity; you can obey his commands and make progress toward that ideal only with the help of his Holy Spirit.
5. Motivation for obedience must be based on an overwhelming gratitude for his costly Gift and an endless appreciation for his amazing and perfect love.

Challenge!

Take a few moments to reflect on God's high standards for purity. Then respond to the following questions:

1. Think about the story of the frog in hot water. Have your standards slipped at all over the years because of the lower standards of the world today? If so, in what specific ways? If not, how has God helped you to avoid that compromise?

_____

_____

_____

2. How do you feel about God's incredibly high standards? Do you agree that his way is ultimately best for you? Why or why not?

_____

_____

_____

3. He knows we can't be perfect, but he wants our hearts to *want* to be perfect. Do you want that as well? Tell him about it.

_____

_____

_____

4. How are you feeling right now about his incredible love for you?

_____

_____

_____

5. What's *your* motivation for being obedient?

_____

_____

_____

Involve God in Your Resolve!

He *does* know best. He is Creator of the universe, yet he loves you as his precious child, his perfect and beautiful little girl!

> *My loving Daddy, help me to see how your expectations for me are really practical guidelines for my happiness. I want to willingly and lovingly obey you. I want to say with the psalmist, "I delight to do your will, my God, for your law is written on my heart!" (Psalm 40:8 TLB). I know I can't do it alone—I need you and your strength. I need the body of Christ around me. Help me to get connected with people who will encourage me and love me just as I am and who, with me, are committed to loving and obeying you. Each day I want to look deeply into your eyes of love and remember how you have loved me and pursued me from the moment of my conception. Thank you, Abba, for loving me so much!*

What else do you want to ask God right now? What else do you want to tell him?

_____

_____

_____

_____

_____

> *I pray this in the name of your precious Son, Jesus. Amen.*

What do you sense he is saying to you right now?

_____

_____

_____

_____

Identify the Opposition

The world, the flesh, and the devil join forces and assault the soul so straitly and so untiringly that, without humble reliance on the ever-present aid of God, they drag the soul down in spite of all resistance.

Brother Lawrence

It's a jungle out there.

It's almost impossible to avoid the traps and snares of the *world* around us.

Worse, inside of us we have this small, selfish, and very demanding entity—our *flesh*—loudly insisting that we act on every whim.

And to top it off, in the unseen but very real spiritual world we have an *enemy* who will do anything he can to trick us into buying into his lies.

These are the adversaries we face. You've heard the expression, "Know your enemy," and there is wisdom in that. So we're going to get acquainted with our spiritual foes, and we'll begin with the big one.

The Enemy of Our Souls

Make no mistake. Satan is real and he's out to destroy. He would love nothing more than to convince us that there are plenty of solutions apart from God for getting our needs met. He is sly, he is vicious, and he is a liar. He will promise anything—undying love and adoration, feelings of great worth and importance, overwhelming happiness—anything to draw us into his grasp.

God's Word tells us that "the devil . . . was a murderer from the beginning, not holding to the truth, for there is no truth in him. When he lies, he speaks his native language, for he is a liar and the father of lies" (John 8:44). He is the author of discouragement, condemnation, worry, hatred, confusion, anxiety, fear, and doubt. And he is devious.

In her book *Battlefield of the Mind*, Joyce Meyer says this about Satan: "He begins by bombarding our mind with a cleverly devised pattern of little nagging thoughts, suspicions, doubts, fears, wonderings, reasonings and theories. He moves slowly and cautiously . . . he has a strategy for his warfare. He has studied us for a long time."[1]

One of Satan's favorite tricks is to mix a bit of his lies with truth. Or evil with what is good. It's the same ruse we use with our cat, Fluffy, or our dog, Bingo—we hide the icky-tasting pill in the middle of the yummy food. It makes it go down easier. I believe that is what is so insidious about cults as well as the New Age and metaphysical movements. So much of what they espouse sounds good and lovely on the surface, even biblical. But many of their doctrines mix truth with beliefs that are not consistent with God's Word. We need to use critical thinking before absorbing assumptions.

Recognize the Enemy

Satan knows where we are most vulnerable. Again, Meyer comments: "He knows what we like and what we don't like. He knows our insecurities, our weaknesses and our fears.

He knows what bothers us most. He is willing to invest any amount of time it takes to defeat us. One of the devil's strong points is patience."[2]

What does this mean for us? We need to be endlessly alert. If you are constantly being reminded that diligent prayer and daily devotions are important for your Christian life and spiritual growth, there's a good reason. Just consider how Satan is patiently lurking, looking for an opening, and that reminder becomes a "No duh!" The moment we let our guard down, Satan is there, ready to pounce.

It's not always easy. At least it hasn't been for me. Once you take a stand for God, Satan will try everything, every angle he can. You are now a threat! You may recognize the cycle I typically experience. Once I determine to give up something for God, the battle begins. The bigger and tougher the commitment, the bigger the battle. Then, about the time I think I have it conquered, it comes back even bigger and stronger.

The struggle doesn't go away; we just get better at letting God manage it with us. But Satan and his hordes are like a pack of hungry, snarling wolves, circling, looking for the weakest spot. So remember, as you get stronger, he gets more devious!

We are in a *war*—a spiritual battle—and we are *behind enemy lines*! So "be careful—watch out for attacks from Satan, your great enemy. He prowls around like a hungry, roaring lion, looking for some victim to tear apart. Stand firm when he attacks. Trust the Lord; and remember that other Christians all around the world are going through these sufferings too" (1 Peter 5:8–9 TLB).

I love the way author Paul Thigpen puts it: "That prowling, hungry lion is out there today. The choice is clear: Be armed—or be breakfast."[3]

Victory in Jesus

Jesus's resurrection was a critical blow to Satan. The enemy was defeated. So, as Neil Anderson questions in his book *The*

Bondage Breaker, "If Satan is already disarmed, why don't we experience more victory in our lives? . . . [He looks ferocious but] in reality, his fangs have been removed and he has been declawed, but if he can deceive you into believing that he can chew you up and spit you out, he can control your behavior, which is just what he wants to do."[4]

When we experience spiritual attack, we must remind ourselves that we have the Holy Spirit living inside us, and that God is far greater than Satan (1 John 4:4). But I want to remind you "that your strength must come from the Lord's mighty power within you. Put on all of God's armor so that you will be able to stand safe against all strategies and tricks of Satan. For we are not fighting against people made of flesh and blood, but against persons without bodies—the evil rulers of the unseen world, those mighty satanic beings and great evil princes of darkness who rule this world; and against huge numbers of wicked spirits in the spirit world" (Ephesians 6:10–12 TLB).

We need to submit ourselves to God and resist the devil. When we do that, he will flee from us (see James 4:7). We can say to ourselves, "It is true that I am an ordinary, weak human being, but I don't use human plans and methods to win my battles. I use God's mighty weapons, not those made by men, to knock down the devil's strongholds. These weapons can break down every proud argument against God" (2 Corinthians 10:3–5 TLB).

Focus on Jesus

One more thing. Even though there are evil spiritual beings out there, don't start looking for demons under every rock. *What we focus on we give power to.* If you feel like you are experiencing an attack, *focus on Jesus.* Our primary defense is prayer, asking God to protect and strengthen us. Be prepared in advance by studying God's Word and learning more about the enemy. Memorize Scripture so you have it handy when you need it. Put on the armor of God. Rely on Christian friends for encouragement and words of truth. And trust God to be with you.

The Last Laugh

In our quest for living for God, it may help us to stop and realize that Satan *despises* our commitment to be holy and pure and *laughs* at our failures. When I am sometimes feeling weak or discouraged and tempted to give up or give in, I remind myself that he is snickering at me. That gets my hackles up. That restores my resolve to "do it for God"! And I can also know that God, after all, has the last laugh.

The World

I remember being at the beach as a small child. Clear blue sky. White-crested breakers gently rolling into shore. I loved standing on the wet sand near the water's edge, waiting for the last little remnant of a wave to reach my feet. It came toward me, a soft, lacy frill of white foam on the leading edge. I vividly recall the feeling of the sand trickling away beneath my feet as it flowed in past my ankles. As the tide receded, even more sand would swirl away, and I would be left standing in a shallow indentation filled with seawater, my feet partially buried in sand.

As lovely a picture as that paints, it's also a good illustration of how evil in the world operates. It constantly works to erode our spiritual foundation from beneath us. Sometimes it acts as a tiny current, removing a few grains of sand at a time. At other times, hitting like a tsunami, it knocks our knees out from under us. But even a small trickle, allowed to continue, can ultimately carve a deep gouge in a granite boulder.

We need to guard ourselves against *anything* that pulls our affections away from God, and there's plenty out there that will try to do just that! It's not easy. We are told to be *in* the world but not *of* the world. We're not to crawl away and hide from the world. Instead, we are called to live right here in the middle of it. We literally have to put ourselves in harm's way.

We face a twofold challenge in the world. On the one hand, we have to stand strong and fight against the things that compromise our walk with Christ. That alone is a test. And then on the other hand, when we are living lives that honor God, even in the face of tough obstacles, that means we look different. We don't blend in. We stand out. As with typical human behavior, when the world sees its own sin in contrast to purity, we are loathed for it. That is why Jesus said, "If you belonged to the world, it would love you as its own. As it is, you do not belong to the world, but I have chosen you out of the world. That is why the world hates you" (John 15:19).

To avoid corruption by the world we need to do our utmost to (1) avoid the patterns and behaviors of the world, and (2) firmly plant God's truth in our minds.

So "do not conform any longer to the pattern of this world, but be transformed by the renewing of your mind. Then you will be able to test and approve what God's will is—his good, pleasing and perfect will" (Romans 12:2). As we lean on him—and not try to tackle the world by ourselves—his Holy Spirit will renew, reeducate, and redirect our minds until we are truly transformed.[5]

But as this miraculous transformation is taking place, our "old self" is constantly warring with our new, spiritually reborn self.

The Old Nature

"We have met the enemy and he is us."

This well-known quote comes from an old cartoon strip called *Pogo*. And truer words were never spoken, even though they were said in jest. Sometimes we are our own worst enemy.

Before we accepted Christ as our Savior, we were operating from our "flesh" or our "lower nature." We felt we were in charge and pretty much did the best we could, based on the values we adopted for ourselves. Basically, we were living for ourselves instead of for God.

Well-known author Elisabeth Elliot, in *Discipline: The Glad Surrender,* explains: "Paul spells out exactly what the lower nature is. It is all that is against God. 'For the outlook of the lower nature is enmity with God.' 'That nature sets its desires against the Spirit.'"[6]

Sometimes we are our own worst enemy.

When we accept Christ as our Savior, that old self is put to death. We have been "crucified with Christ," and we ourselves no longer live, but Christ lives in us (Galatians 2:20). We are given new life in him. A new self.

But that doesn't mean the old, selfish self doesn't continue to assert itself! When I listen closely, in my head I can hear the voice of a little two-year-old girl, whining and begging to get what *she* wants, even though I'm trying to watch my weight: "But I *waaaant* ice cream!" When turning from the temptation of watching a funny, but lewd, show on TV, it's the voice of a spoiled preadolescent, insisting she get to do what *she* wants: "Come onnnn! *EVERYone* watches it! It's not *thaaat* bad! And no one will know! *Pleeeeeze*??"

But that old nature will drag us down if we allow it. It will continue to demand its own way, rather than giving up earthly desires in order to please God. "You were taught, with regard to your former way of life, to put off your old self, which is being corrupted by its deceitful desires; to be made new in the attitude of your minds; and to put on the new self, created to be like God in true righteousness and holiness" (Ephesians 4:22–24).

We are told to "put to death, therefore, whatever belongs to your earthly nature: sexual immorality, impurity, lust, evil desires and greed, which is idolatry" (Colossians 3:5) and are encouraged with the knowledge that we, "however, are controlled *not* by the sinful nature but by the Spirit, if the Spirit of God lives in you" (Romans 8:9, emphasis mine). And since we have the Holy Spirit in us, he will guide us in living our lives the right way, if we will listen. "I advise you to obey only the Holy Spirit's instructions. He will tell you where to go and what to do, and then you won't always be doing the wrong things your *evil nature* wants you to. For we naturally love to do evil things that are just the opposite from the things that the Holy Spirit tells us to do; and the good things we want to do when the Spirit has his way with us are just the opposite of our *natural desires*. These two forces within us are constantly fighting each other to win control over us, and our wishes are never free from their pressures" (Galatians 5:16–17 TLB, emphasis mine).

God Is Patient

So often I wonder why God doesn't just give up on me. It seems like every time I turn around, I flounder. I determine to change things that need changing, then, oops, there I go again! Soon I start feeling like a failure as a Christian. Does that ever happen to you?

At those times we need to remind ourselves that we're still human. Look at the apostle Paul. Talk about a godly man. And yet he struggled in the same way we do. He says about himself,

> I find this law at work: When I want to do good, evil is right there with me. For in my inner being I delight in God's law; but I see another law at work in the members of my body, waging war against the law of my mind and making me a prisoner of the law of sin at work within my members. *What a wretched man I am! Who will rescue me from this body of death? Thanks be to God—through Jesus Christ our Lord!*

So then, I myself in my mind am a slave to God's law, but in the sinful nature a slave to the law of sin.

Romans 7:21–25, emphasis mine

I don't know about you, but that tells me I want to avoid being in the sinful nature—I don't want to be a slave to sin. That means we have to give up things our flesh doesn't want us to give up, but it beats being in bondage!

So how do we experience more success in this effort? Obviously, we need to ask God for his strength and wisdom. But it also requires discipline and self-control on our part.

Self-Control

In his book *The Practice of Godliness*, Jerry Bridges says this:

> Self-control is necessary *because* we are at war with our own sinful desires. James describes those desires as dragging us away and enticing us into sin (1:14). Peter says they war against our own souls (1 Peter 2:11). Paul speaks of them as deceitful (Ephesians 4:22). What makes these sinful desires so dangerous is that *they dwell within our own heart.* External temptations would not be nearly so dangerous were it not for the fact that they find this ally of desire right within our own breast.[7]

Self-control is necessary for our defense and safety. The Old Testament tells us that a person without self-control is as defenseless as a city with the outer walls of protection broken down (see Proverbs 25:28). And that "wall" in my life, just like those old stone fortifications, is what protects me from the enemy. So my prayer is that Jesus will help me rebuild my wall of self-control, stone by stone, until it is in good repair. I want this because I know that the person with self-control is mightier than she who conquers a city (see

Proverbs 16:32). I don't want to be like "those who let themselves be controlled by their lower natures [and] live only to please themselves, but [instead I want to be like] those who follow after the Holy Spirit [and] find themselves doing those things that please God" (Romans 8:5 TLB). As we choose to deny the selfish internal desires and realize the old sinful nature has no real power over us, we can live our lives with more genuine freedom and joy.

Warning: Guard Your Mind

"Sin is sin." That's what my pastor told me as we were discussing my battles with The Beast. He went on to say that we all struggle and we all sin, and that to God, every sin—big or little—translates as rebellion against God. Then he said something I've never forgotten:

"It all starts between the ears."

Hmmm. Hadn't really thought about that before, but it made sense. Before anything ever happens, we *think* about it. And as we're told in Proverbs 23:7, "For as he thinketh in his heart, so is he" (KJV). Pretty powerful. If what merely starts in our minds can lead us into sin, maybe we'd better pay special attention to what we're letting into our minds.

Oswald Chambers says, "We have to remember that our conscious life, even though only a small part of our total person, is to be regarded by us as a 'temple of the Holy Spirit.' He will be responsible for the unconscious part which we don't know, but we must pay careful attention to and guard the conscious part for which we are responsible."[8]

If we allow our enemies to control our minds, they can control us!

The "Big 3"—and Then Some

Satan, the world, and the flesh. These are the "Big 3" opponents that together try to drag us away from God's truth and his intended love for our lives. But unfortunately, the opposition doesn't stop there.

There are two other enemies that deflate our spiritual passion, take the edge off our appetite for God, and reduce our effectiveness for his kingdom: spiritual complacency and self-contentment.

Spiritual Complacency

In this worldly spiritual conflict, Satan is not worried about Christians who are "prisoners of war." They're no threat. He has them right where he wants them—removed from the battle. Ineffective. Powerless. It's only when we're standing for God that the devil takes offense. Complacency takes us out of the game.

In this worldly spiritual conflict, Satan is not worried about Christians who are "prisoners of war."

If we allow ourselves to become indifferent about Christ, we hurt both him and ourselves. We hurt Christ because we are wasting a life that he redeemed with a great price. We hurt ourselves because we are living in mediocrity instead of living out God-sized lives.

God despises spiritual complacency. He looks inside of us. If our faith is wishy-washy, he says, "I know your deeds, that you are neither cold nor hot. I wish you were either one or the other! So, because you are lukewarm—neither hot nor cold—I am about to spit you out of my mouth. You say, 'I am rich; I have acquired wealth and do not need a thing.' But you do not realize that you are wretched, pitiful, poor, blind and naked" (Revelation 3:15–17). He wants us to *take a stand for him*—to be counted among those who are passionate about him.

Self-Contentment

There is one more enemy, one to which we are exceptionally vulnerable here in America: self-contentment.

When God's good gifts to us become more important than God himself, we choke God out of our lives.

> Jesus said some people hear the word of God, and a desire for God is awakened in their hearts. But then, "as they go on their way they are choked with worries and riches and pleasures of this life" (Luke 8:14). In another place he said, "The desires for other things enter in and choke the word, and it becomes unfruitful" (Mark 4:19). The "pleasures of this life" and "the desires for other things"—these are not evil in themselves. These are not the vices. These are gifts of God. They are your basic meat and potatoes and coffee and gardening and reading and decorating and traveling and investing and TV-watching and Internet-surfing and shopping and exercising and collecting and talking. And all of them can become deadly substitutes for God.[9]

So says John Piper in his book *A Hunger for God.*

Although there is nothing inherently wrong with any of these things, if we unwittingly let them fill every crevice of our lives and our beings, we leave little room for God. Piper continues:

> The greatest enemy of hunger for God is not poison but apple pie. It is not the banquet of the wicked that dulls our appetite for heaven, but endless nibbling at the table of the world. It is not the X-rated video, but the prime-time dribble of triviality we drink in every night. For all the ill that Satan can do, when God describes what keeps us from the banquet table of his love, it is a piece of land, a yoke of oxen, and a wife (Luke 14:18–20). The greatest adversary of love to God is not his enemies but his gifts. And the most deadly appetites are not for the poison of evil, but for the simple pleasures of earth. For when these

replace an appetite for God himself, the idolatry is scarcely recognizable, and almost incurable.[10]

As we seek to grow closer to God, and especially as we look to him to fulfill our needs, we have to be careful lest his very gifts to us become a replacement for him. We must lift them up to him with thanksgiving, acknowledging that they are given to us, by him, in love. And we must vow to renew our love, our passion, and our hunger for him, the Giver of all gifts.

Reminder

It is good to remember that we belong to God. He lives in us! Nothing and no one can take that from us. We're not in this war alone. Jesus has already conquered Satan and the sin of this world. And "I pray that you will begin to understand how incredibly great his power is to help those who believe him. It is that same mighty power that raised Christ from the dead and seated him in the place of honor at God's right hand in heaven" (Ephesians 1:19–20 TLB).

Chapter Summary

Step 6: Identify the Opposition

1. In Christ, you already have victory over your enemies—but you must know it, believe it, and act on it.
2. To be effective in the battle against the world, Satan, and your old nature, you must be alert, understand their tactics, and be armed and prepared.
3. Satan is relentless, and your passions are often where he will look for an opening; guard your affections and take every thought captive.
4. If the enemy can keep you inside the fence as a prisoner of war, you and your faith are no threat to him; complacency is his friend.
5. Sometimes God's greatest gifts can be our biggest struggle; let him have first place over *everything* in your life.

Challenge!

Are you beginning to see how you can live life with victory? And that with victory comes pure joy and fulfillment? Read and respond to the following questions.

1. Are you ever tempted to let inappropriate or sinful thoughts "simmer" in your mind? What kinds of thoughts? How might those thoughts affect your heart toward God?

_____

_____

_____

2. Are you inside or outside the prison compound of your old nature? Where do you want to be? Why?

_____

_____

_____

_____

3. After reading about the craftiness of our enemy, are you sensing a need to be better armed? If so, what can you do?

_____

_____

_____

_____

4. Look at the following "Who Am I?" chart. As you read, where do you see yourself? What are your thoughts? Is there anything you want to do differently? What? Why?

_____

_____

_____

_____

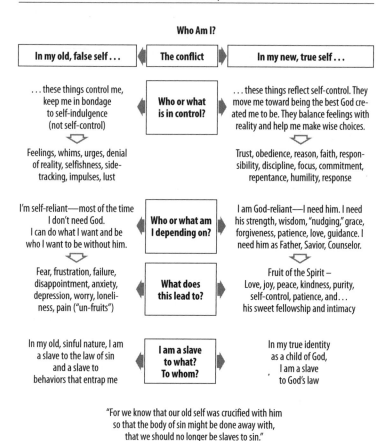

Who Am I?

In my old, false self ...	The conflict	In my new, true self ...
... these things control me, keep me in bondage to self-indulgence (not self-control)	**Who or what is in control?**	... these things reflect self-control. They move me toward being the best God created me to be. They balance feelings with reality and help me make wise choices.
Feelings, whims, urges, denial of reality, selfishness, side-tracking, impulses, lust		Trust, obedience, reason, faith, responsibility, discipline, focus, commitment, repentance, humility, response
I'm self-reliant—most of the time I don't need God. I can do what I want and be who I want to be without him.	**Who or what am I depending on?**	I am God-reliant—I need him. I need his strength, wisdom, "nudging," grace, forgiveness, patience, love, guidance. I need him as Father, Savior, Counselor.
Fear, frustration, failure, disappointment, anxiety, depression, worry, loneliness, pain ("un-fruits")	**What does this lead to?**	Fruit of the Spirit – Love, joy, peace, kindness, purity, self-control, patience, and... his sweet fellowship and intimacy
In my old, sinful nature, I am a slave to the law of sin and a slave to behaviors that entrap me	**I am a slave to what? To whom?**	In my true identity as a child of God, I am a slave to God's law

"For we know that our old self was crucified with him
so that the body of sin might be done away with,
that we should no longer be slaves to sin."
– Romans 6:6

Involve God in Your Resolve!

God has already won the battle! You can know that he is standing right beside you as you fight yours.

Almighty God, my Rock and my Fortress, I'm so grateful I don't have to live my life here on earth without you. It is so overwhelming at times, and I often feel attacked on every side. Teach me what I need to learn about my enemies, but lead me to focus on you rather than on the struggle. Help me to know when to flee, like Joseph fled from Potiphar's wife (see Genesis 39:1–12) and when to stand strong. I will pray to you without ceasing, because I know you hear my prayers and they delight you. Do what I cannot, Lord. My only confidence and competence comes from you (2 Corinthians 3:5). Thank you, precious Lord, that you are my ever-watchful Shepherd and my mighty Shield. With your loving protection, I have nothing and no one to fear!

What else do you want to ask God right now? What else do you want to tell him?

_____

_____

_____

_____

_____

I pray this in the name of your precious Son, Jesus. Amen.

What do you sense he is saying to you right now?

_____

_____

_____

_____

======= Step 7 =======

Understand Your Design

> You made all the delicate, inner parts of my body, and knit them together in my mother's womb. Thank you for making me so wonderfully complex!
>
> Psalm 139:13–14 TLB

Here's something profound to consider: Our actions, thoughts, and attitudes will ultimately reflect what we *truly* believe.

Think about it. Have you ever had a bad hair day? How does that impact the way you carry yourself? The confidence with which you meet and greet other people? The way you see yourself? Or if you're one of those incredibly fortunate women who never experiences disobedient hair, then how about a ketchup spill on the front of your blouse just before an important meeting? Or a zit on the end of your nose right before your high school reunion?

We care about how we look. And caring is fine, as long as we don't confuse it with worth and value. But listen to the words we say to ourselves in these circumstances: "This looks terrible! No one will take me seriously. I look like an idiot. I look ugly! How can I hide this? She's going to look so much better than I do. I can't complete with her when I look like this. People will look down on me. I won't be seen as beautiful . . . professional . . . polished . . . perfect."

Okay, so we have a hair, wardrobe, or complexion challenge. But we haven't changed. Our worth hasn't diminished. Yet somehow we allow the tiniest of things to warp the truth of who we are. Can you relate to this? It starts with a perception—right or wrong—and blossoms into a very convincing internal dialogue we call *self-talk*. Unlike our verbal conversations, our self-talk is pretty much nonstop. And if we allow negative, unproductive, or untrue thoughts to run rampant through our minds, they frame our behaviors and thoughts.

Our Design

As a college student exploring the complexity of the human body, I often wondered how anyone could not believe in God as the Creator. The more I learned, the more I was impressed with the intricacies that make up our beings. Our anatomy alone is astounding, but when interlinked with our physiology, sociology, and psychology, the human body is mind boggling. Add to that our spiritual nature, and it becomes apparent just how magnificently we are fashioned. And God is the Master Designer of it all.

You may think I'm switching gears here, but I'm not. We've been talking about how our thoughts (psychological selves) impact our actions (sociological selves, or our human behavior). Our physiology is what ties it all together and makes us function in the way we were designed to function. Our connection with God provides our true purpose, our true identity, and our uniqueness as his special creation. Here on earth, our bodies, our minds, and our spiritual selves are inseparable.

As a result, what we *really* believe and what we say to ourselves significantly impact our actions. That being the case, it just might be important for us to give some thought to what we think. And if our thinking is not based on God's truth, or if it is negative and nonproductive, then what?

Let's start with a basic but important question.

Events, Thoughts, Actions

Do people, situations, difficulties, and temptations determine the way we feel? What do you think? I have found that the great majority of people say yes. But I want to challenge that belief. Are people, situations, difficulties, and temptations truly what determine the way we feel, or is it our *interpretation* of people, situations, difficulties, and temptations that determines the way we feel?

Think about it. Have you ever been in a situation where you reacted one way and a friend reacted another? Most people have.

I remember a time a friend and I were out for lunch and afterward were heading home on a busy street. We were chatting away when a car on my right swerved and almost ran into me. It was obvious the driver hadn't seen me until the last minute and then managed to pull back into her own lane before actually hitting us. Based purely on my own interpretation of her wild gyrations, the other driver was saying, "I'm so sorry! What a doofus I am! I can't believe I just did that!" It cracked me up. I started laughing. My friend, on the other hand, got angry. She launched into a tirade about lousy, inconsiderate drivers.

Same circumstance. Different reactions.

Now let's look at a simple physiological model that explains this.

We see that when we experience a *trigger*—an immediate person, situation, or difficulty that causes us to react—that experience is processed through our *filter*—our mental interpretive database that is based on our beliefs and perceptions.

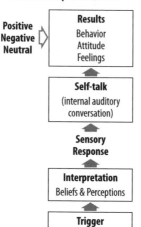

Stimulus-Response Reaction

Those perceptions then create *self-talk*—that little voice inside our heads—which then directly influences our resulting behavior, attitudes, and feelings.

So, does that mean that we are merely automatons, with no real control over our thoughts and our ultimate reactions? Not at all. We have a *choice* as to how we respond to people and circumstances around us. It begins with a desire to please God, to change and grow, to get different results than we've been getting, and to alter our nonproductive habits.

And here's the bonus. As we begin to consciously change and improve our self-talk, not only will we begin to experience improved thoughts and behaviors, we will notice our perceptions changing as well.

Old Nature, New Nature

When we are faced with challenges, whether they are temptations or undesired circumstances, we have a *choice*. We can allow our old flesh nature to control us. Or we can choose to challenge our perceptions and self-talk by holding them up to the Word of God—his truth and his promises.

Let's look at the same model but with additional and more sophisticated information added.

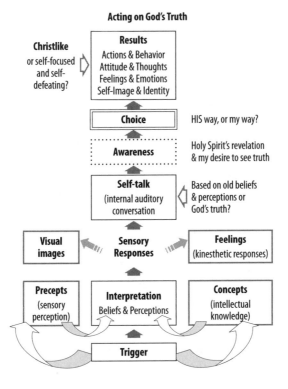

Triggers, Filters, and Perceptions

You'll notice that we added "Awareness" and "Choice" to the equation. And so you'll be really impressed, we also included some scientific-sounding zings and do-dahs.

Let's go back to the beginning by examining the trigger. A *trigger* is anything that causes a reaction in us. It may be mild or intense. It may be positive or negative. But it affects us. We view the immediate situation based on our intellectual knowledge, our feelings. Other senses pick up additional cues. All of that is fed into our "filtration system" and interpreted through our existing beliefs and perceptions. *Everything* gets filtered.

Now we have to stop here and ask, Where do our beliefs and perceptions come from? If we could brainstorm together, we would come up with a list that includes things like parents, friends, teachers, church, past experiences, pastors, the media, values taught to us, and so on. But can we assume that ALL of that input is correct? Probably not! But based on all of that input, we have formulated certain beliefs, and we tend to think that what *we* believe is correct.

If you were bitten by a dog or maybe were just badly frightened by one as an impressionable young child, you may have grown up with a fear of dogs. ALL dogs, big or small. Is that logical? Is it true that all dogs are dangerous? No, but it may be true for you until something changes that perception.

Perceptions and beliefs directly lead to the end results we get.

More important, if you were raised by a loving daddy who believed you were a wonderful, beautiful little girl, you're going to have a very different perception of yourself than a young girl who got nothing but derisive, derogatory feedback from her father or no feedback at all. The truth is, we are all worthy of love from a loving Father, but for some that is easier to believe than for others. In that case, the negative perception needs to be corrected.

Bottom line, perceptions and beliefs directly lead to the end results we get. When they are correct, positive, and based on God's truth, they are invaluable to our well-being. Unfortunately, in this fallen world we have been fed a lot of untruths that directly or indirectly result in unproductive and negative actions, attitudes, beliefs, feelings, and self-images.

Sensory Responses

As information filters through our beliefs and perceptions, our minds primarily respond with three types of sensory experiences:

1. We create mind pictures, or visual images.
2. We experience feelings and emotions.
3. And we frame our self-talk, that little conversation inside our heads.

Here is a critically important point: Our minds cannot differentiate between what is real and what is imagined. It's true! If we create or perceive a detailed, sensory-rich experience, our brains interpret it as real.[1] Case in point: look how real many movies seem. They are designed to create an experience as close to reality as possible—sound effects, music, color, focus, emotion. That's why we can watch a movie for the second time and still cry or be frightened. They make an experience seem *real* to our minds. So it is in this very arena of sensory images that we need to challenge ourselves.

Take Captive Every Thought

God knows how powerful our senses are. He made them. It's our job to line them up with his truth, especially in matters of the heart. Solomon warns us that above all else, we are to guard our affections because they influence everything else in our lives (see Proverbs 4:23).

Sometimes we focus on a "reality" that is based on a lie. We may have experienced hurt at the hands of another that has us doubting our value, our worthiness, our lovability. But if we replay the associated images, self-talk, and feelings over and over, we are ingraining the lies as truth.

If we create a false "reality" for ourselves, such as with a fantasy or an infatuation, with repetition it will become more

119

and more real in our minds. And the more real it seems, the more likely we are to act on it.

Self-Talk

Do you talk to yourself? If you found yourself saying, "No, I don't talk to myself" . . . you just did! We all do. It's normal. Mostly we don't notice it, unless we talk to ourselves out loud. Which maybe isn't normal, but then again, I do it!

Self-talk is potent stuff. If we are feeding ourselves primarily healthy, positive words, we will most likely experience positive thoughts and behaviors. However, if we are ingesting mostly unhealthy, untrue information, that internal verbal diet will eventually tear us down. Think of it this way. What we plant, grows. If you want a beautiful, green lawn, you won't plant weed seeds.

The scary thing is, experts tell us that 75 percent or more of this nonstop chatter is negative or counterproductive. That is why it is so critical that we learn to identify and then modify pessimistic, sinful, or inaccurate self-talk. When we do, we can actually begin to change outcomes. If our self-talk isn't consistent with God's truth or his requirements for obedience, we have the option to change it.

But first we have to become *aware* of what we're saying to ourselves.

Awareness

Awareness of some kind always precedes a desired change, and change requires both a choice and a commitment. If we see no need for change, we won't be motivated to do anything differently. But because most of us want to grow with God and become more like the women he designed us to be, we need to become aware of what's going on inside our heads—our self-talk.

120

The Holy Spirit will help us do just that. We can pray and ask him to disclose our wrong thinking. "Search me, O God, and know my heart; test my thoughts. Point out anything you find in me that makes you sad, and lead me along the path of everlasting life" (Psalm 139:23–24 TLB). As we pray and read God's Word, he will reveal to us those things he wants to change. And as we become aware of what is negative, untrue, unhealthy, or unproductive in our minds, we then have a choice to make.

Choice

Here is one of God's greatest gifts: choice! That divine gift that allows us the freedom to do with our lives what we want. Think about it. If God hadn't given us freedom of choice, and instead made all of us little Stepford women who would love him and serve him and do his will, would that be love and obedience? No. He wants our love for him to be real. And he wants our obedience to be voluntary because of our love. Otherwise it means nothing.

His truth is there for us to see—in his Word, and in our hearts when we are open to his leading. And when we are confronted with truth, our hearts either soften in submission to his touch or harden in stubbornness and rebellion.

In order to be truly happy, we need to make good choices. Sin hurts us and grieves God. Even when faced with highly emotional choices, we must be responsible and act according to God's desires, not our own. Christ's death on the cross freed us from sin, so sin has no authority over us. But we must practice self-discipline to say no to what is wrong.

And the first step in disciplining our lives for obedience begins with *choosing* to examine and renew our thought life—our self-talk. "Do not conform any longer to the pattern of this world, but be transformed by the *renewing of your mind*" (Romans 12:2, emphasis mine). As we do this repeatedly, we will begin to see a difference—in our thoughts, our feelings, and our behaviors.

Results

"A [woman] reaps what [she] sows" (Galatians 6:7), and this is true in regard to what we allow in our minds. "The one who sows to please [her] sinful nature, from that nature will reap destruction; the one who sows to please the Spirit, from the Spirit will reap eternal life" (Galatians 6:8). As we choose to correct our negative or incorrect self-talk—and replace it with God's truth and goodness—we will reap the benefits of a more joyful outlook and an increased understanding of God's endless love for us.

That sounds like a great choice to me! How about you?

Chapter Summary

Step 7: Understand Your Design

1. Your real beliefs and perceptions are demonstrated in your actions and words.
2. Your perceptions and beliefs—not people, events, challenges, and circumstances—cause you to feel what you feel.
3. Your mind is so amazingly designed that it cannot distinguish between what is real and what is realistically presented; therefore, it is very important what you allow into your mind.
4. What you put in your mind is ultimately what you will see in your results.

Challenge!

1. As you walked through the models, did you think about some of the ways you may blame people and circumstances for your feelings?

   _____

   _____

   _____

   _____

2. Did you identify any triggers that set off undesired responses? If so, what are they?

   _____

   _____

   _____

   _____

3. What are your thoughts about the importance of choice in the way we frame our self-talk?

   _____

   _____

   _____

   _____

4. Can you think of any negative or unproductive self-talk you might have that will be really difficult to change? If so, what is it? Why will it be difficult to change? How can God help you with that?

_____

_____

_____

_____

Involve God in Your Resolve!

God has given you a unique and highly sophisticated mind. Praise him for the wonders of his creation—you!

Oh Lord, the more I learn about myself as your creation, the more amazed I am. Thank you for helping me understand some of the intricacies of my mind and for providing me with knowledge I can use to cultivate positive and godly thinking. I know that as I nurture what is good and pleasing to you, I will see growth in my life. I desire to please you; and I know that as I take the initiative to do what is right, you will give me the strength and wisdom to do it. How marvelous you are! With the psalmist I pray, "Create in me a clean heart, O God, and renew a right, persevering, and steadfast spirit within me" (Psalm 51:10 AMP). I will work as if it's all up to me, and pray as if it's all up to you, knowing full well that you will do your good work in me. Thank you, Father!

What else do you want to ask God right now? What else do you want to tell him?

_____

_____

_____

_____

_____

I pray this in the name of your precious Son, Jesus. Amen.

What do you sense he is saying to you right now?

_____

_____

_____

_____

Choose to Follow God

Those who live according to the sinful nature have their minds set on what that nature desires; but those who live in accordance with the Spirit have their minds set on what the Spirit desires.

Romans 8:5

"Hmmm . . . what to wear today . . ."

"Should I get the low-cal Chinese chicken salad, or should I splurge and get that juicy burger with bacon and cheese—and maybe fries on the side?"

"Wow. A whole Friday evening to myself! Do I want to stay up and watch a video or curl up in bed with a good book?"

Choices. We make them all day, every day. Big ones, little ones. Important ones and inconsequential ones. Choices like what time to get up in the morning and whether or not to skip brushing our teeth "just for tonight." Choices like deciding about a new car or considering a move clear across the country.

And many of our choices have significant consequences. If we turn off our alarm and roll over for a few more minutes of sleep, we may be late for work. If we buy a brand-new car, it's likely we will have a new monthly financial obligation.

God gives us freedom of choice. Freedom to do things his way or to do them our way. And there are consequences for our choices, good and bad.

Bad Apples

Remember Adam and Eve in the garden? They made a choice—to believe a self-serving lie rather than God's loving truth. As a result, sin is rampant in the world today. Personally, I'd like to go back in time and smack Eve—but then I realize it could just as well have been me who ate that apple! In fact, I've probably eaten enough of those "apples" in my lifetime to rival seventeen years of apple production for the state of Washington.

God's Word is pretty clear about choosing his way or our way. It may sound harsh unless we remind ourselves that his motive is love. Just as a parent takes a stance with life-impacting rules, God, too, emphasizes those things that cause us to fall into danger. And just as a loving parent enforces discipline—consequences for infractions—God allows us to experience the consequences of our behavior. Not only is he loving, he is also just.

Scripture reflects choices and consequences. Here are a few that demonstrate outcomes of *poor* choices:

CHOICE	CONSEQUENCE
"You must not eat from the tree of the knowledge of good and evil . . .	. . . when you eat of it you will surely die."
	Genesis 2:17
"They became fools and exchanged the glory of the immortal God for images. . . .	Therefore God gave them over in the sinful desires of their hearts."
	Romans 1:22–24

CHOICE	CONSEQUENCE
"Since they did not think it worthwhile to retain the knowledge of God . . .	. . . he gave them over to a depraved mind." Romans 1:28
"But for those who are self-seeking and who reject the truth and follow evil . . .	. . . there will be wrath and anger." Romans 2:8

In contrast we are shown the results of *Christlike* choices—choices that are founded on the desire to do the right thing. Solomon, the wisest man ever to live, says,

> Every [woman] who listens to me and obeys my instructions will be given wisdom and good sense. Yes, if you want better insight and discernment, and are searching for them as you would for lost money or hidden treasure, then wisdom will be given you, and knowledge of God himself; you will soon learn the importance of reverence for the Lord and of trusting him.
>
> For the Lord grants wisdom! His every word is a treasure of knowledge and understanding. He grants good sense to the godly—his saints. He is their shield, protecting them and guarding their pathway. He shows how to distinguish right from wrong, how to find the right decision every time. For wisdom and truth will enter the very center of your being, filling your life with joy.
>
> Proverbs 2:1–9 TLB

Joy. Isn't that what we all want?

So we get to choose. Will it be our way, based on our feeble knowledge and strength? Or God's way, with his promise of wisdom, good results, and joy? We need to remind ourselves about our adversaries—the world, our flesh, and Satan. They are unrelenting in their attempts to influence us. Are we trusting in our vulnerable selves or in almighty God? Will we do what makes us feel good, or will we resolve to do what God directs us to do, even though it means denying our desires?

Slaves

We are all slaves to something.

"Wait a minute!" you say. "I'm not enslaved to anything . . . am I?" Yes, you are. So am I. If we allow anything or anyone to have control over us, we give that person or thing power. And we are thus enslaved. It may be an overt habit or addiction, like alcohol or power or busyness. It may simply be "self." Bottom line, we are slaves either to sin or to God. In Romans we are told, "Don't you realize that you can choose your own master? You can choose sin (with death) or else obedience (with acquittal). The one to whom you offer yourself—he will take you and be your master and you will be his slave" (Romans 6:16 TLB).

Hmm . . . let me think. Whom do I choose for the role of "Master"? Jesus or my enemy Satan? I choose Jesus!

We all say we want Jesus and his easy yoke as our Master, but when we constantly disobey God, we are giving control back to the enemy.

Disobedience

Disobedience is "doing it our way." Listening to the voices we want to hear. Responding to the desires of our old sinful nature. Ignoring God's Word. "The letter [of Jude] paints a picture of people who live by fantasy and appetite, showing contempt for authority. . . . They live by instinct, like unreasoning beasts, like clouds driven by a wind, trees without fruit, raging waves of the sea, producing only 'the spume of their own shameful deeds,' like stars that follow no orbit, always trying to mold life by their own desires. They are led by emotion and never by the Spirit of God."[1]

This is the result of disobedience. Emptiness and pain. As you read the description, can you feel the futility of it all? Can you see the waste? The shallowness? It reeks of frantic, out-of-control, self-serving lives that are being tossed about with no purpose. In spite of the urgency and the intensity, there is no real love to be found, only meaningless activity. The description "points up the diametrical contrast between the two kingdoms: the one where my will is done and the one where God's will is done. The one that is darkness, the other that is light. And it points to a choice."[2] There's that word again: choice.

Let's look at another out-of-control life. In the book of John we meet a woman who has a checkered past (see John 4:4–30). We hear that she has "had five husbands" and that the man she is now with is not her husband (v. 18). Who is the god in her kingdom? She is. But is she getting her deep needs met by doing it her own way? She obviously believed a man in her life would meet her needs, but after five of them, she was still dissatisfied.

Jesus was her answer. He told her, "Whoever drinks the water I give him will never thirst. Indeed, the water I give him will become in him a spring of water welling up to eternal life" (v. 14).

Fresh, pure spring water. Bubbling up clear, cold, and refreshing. Restoring. Fortifying. Invigorating. Sounds good, doesn't it? Especially when we compare it to the "raging waves of the sea, producing only 'the spume of their own shameful deeds'" that we read about in Jude.

God forgives. People often don't. Sometimes the hardest part is forgiving ourselves. And forgetting.

Don't be misled by God's loving and abundant grace. "God cannot be mocked. A man reaps what he sows. The one who sows to please his sinful nature, from that nature will reap destruction; the one who sows to please the Spirit, from the Spirit will reap eternal life" (Galatians 6:7–8).

God forgives. People often don't. Sometimes the hardest part is forgiving ourselves. And forgetting. The videotapes remain in our minds always, and Satan loves to replay them for us. And that is painful.

Sin leads to painful things—idols, bondage, lack of peace, broken relationships, and more. When we disobey repeatedly, we become habituated to sin. And then the battle back is tough.

Obedience and the Path to Spiritual Growth

Obedience is the path to developing and maturing our "new self." Our old self has been done away with, but we've been living with it for so long that it's hard to give up. We keep listening to it and inviting it back. As we obey God, he is able to transform us. "We have to deliver ourselves from our individuality. This means offering our natural life to God and sacrificing it to Him, so He may transform it into spiritual life through our obedience."[3]

Obedience Leads to Joy

"If you obey my commands, you will remain in my love, just as I have obeyed my Father's commands and remain in his love. I have told you this so that my joy may be in you and that your joy may be complete" (John 15:10–11). Did you catch that? Love! Complete joy! Sounds wonderful, doesn't it? Another verse puts it this way: "But if anyone obeys his word, God's love is truly made complete in him" (1 John 2:5).

Not only does our obedience produce love; our love produces obedience.

But love and obedience work both ways. *Not only does our obedience produce love; our love produces obedience.*

As we consider all God has done for us, our greatest gift back to him is our love. And guess what? As we feel our love for him welling up in our souls, we will be compelled to obey him. We can *say* we love him, but "*this* is love: that we walk in obedience to his commands" (2 John 1:6, emphasis mine).

The world tells us to love until the feelings go away. God tells us his love is everlasting. We are to love him *anyway*—whether the feelings are present or not. This means we need to become selfless—more concerned with pleasing him than pleasing ourselves. This decision is the "beginning of the end."

End of Self

"I myself no longer live, but Christ lives in me. And the *real* life I now have within this body is a result of my trusting in the Son of God, who loved me and gave himself for me" (Galatians 2:20 TLB, emphasis mine). This is what it means to "die to self." Making everything God wants more important than what we want. Laying aside our own desires in order to please him.

Romans 12:1 states it this way: "Therefore, I urge you, [sisters], in view of God's mercy, to offer your bodies as living sacrifices, holy and pleasing to God—this is your spiritual act of worship."

This is not a onetime effort. It is an ongoing discipline. As long as we are in these human bodies, we will veer back to self-interests like a moth to a flame. As Rick Warren so aptly puts it in his bestseller *The Purpose Driven Life*, "The problem with a living sacrifice is that it can crawl off the altar, so you may have to resurrender your life fifty times a day."[4]

Relapses

God not only gives us freedom of choice, he gives us a brain so we can make *intelligent* choices. That doesn't mean we always do. When we resolve to obey God in a difficult matter, we usually have a fight on our hands. When we give in and go back to that sin, we allow the enemy to take back ground we fought hard to gain. The struggle can yo-yo back and forth—we regain ground, we lose ground. The pull of the sin can be powerful, but God's pull on our hearts is powerful too. Satan has a way of making his stuff look good—but underneath it all is slavery and death.

If you find yourself in a struggle between the pain of giving up the pleasure of sin and the pain of feeling out of fellowship with Christ, remember this: **your real choice is choosing between** *having pure delight* **in fellowship with Christ, or** *suffering in bondage* **to your lower nature.**

Pruning

As we trust God for his perfection, he begins to make us perfect—and that includes "surgically" removing those things that do not honor him. Just as a vintner prunes his vines so they will come back healthier and stronger, we have to allow God to cut away the deadwood. We may resist and fight, but if we truly desire to be made whole in him, we will eventually lay ourselves in his hands and allow him to do what he must do. It's a process. But as we make the moment-by-moment choices to let him do with us what he will, we begin to understand the necessity of the discomfort—he removes what is unlovely and replaces it with beauty.

The Long and Short of It

When I was in the midst of my addiction, I was opting for instant gratification. But that self-indulgence was building up deep, ongoing pain and consequences for the long haul. Short-term gain, long-term pain.

In contrast, when I chose obedience, I experienced a great deal of anguish in the beginning. But as time passed, the pain was replaced with peace, joy, and fulfillment beyond my imagination. Short-term pain, long-term gain.

That is true for me today. When God reveals something in me that needs changing, the beginning stages are uncomfortable—even painful at times. But if I keep my eye on the prize,

I know the necessary change will ultimately result in more happiness and contentment. The more I kick and scream about what I'm asked to do—or what is thrust upon me—the longer the process takes. And the more foolish I feel afterward!

The world is all about immediate pleasure, going for the gusto. It wants to push away the reality of consequences. The pregnancy after a one-night stand. The alcohol addiction after years of copious binging. The divorce after one indiscretion—which actually began with many small indiscretions. The guilt that follows indulgence in pornography. The lack of passion for real life because the mind is so caught up in the perfection of a fantasy. The broken heart that continues to look for love in all the wrong places.

God is all about long-term gain.

My Determined Purpose . . .

Either way, there's a price to pay.

It's easy to get caught up in emotions and to feel the pain and discontentment. We were created for love and relationship, so when we don't experience those warm, wonderful feelings in our lives, it's natural for us to be drawn toward thoughts and behaviors that will enable us to remove the empty ache. But in actively avoiding discomfort, we're actually ignoring God's plan for our growth. We're also opening ourselves up to *Either way, there's a price to pay.* even more pain: with sin there is usually a very high price to pay.

Walking with God isn't always easy. There is a price to pay with doing it his way, but we know that when we say "Yes!" to him, there is eternal gain that comes with the pain. And what he has in store for us is infinitely better than anything we can plan for ourselves, higher than our greatest dreams or expectations.

Every day we get to choose sin or obedience. The choice is really easy; it's the lessons that come with it that are difficult. But we can rest in the knowledge that there is absolutely no greater joy in life than experiencing God's presence and enjoying his fellowship.

I don't know about you, but in the world of infinite choices, I choose Jesus. And "[my determined purpose is] that I may know Him [that I may progressively become more deeply and intimately acquainted with Him, perceiving, recognizing and understanding the wonders of His Person more strongly and more clearly]" (Philippians 3:10 AMP).

We are in search of *lasting* joy. A *real* solution for our deepest needs. And by now we know that "there is only one Being Who can satisfy the last aching abyss of the human heart, and that is the Lord Jesus Christ."[5] "God is so vastly wonderful, so utterly and completely delightful that He can, without anything other than Himself, meet and overflow the deepest demands of our total nature, mysterious and deep as that nature is."[6]

Whatever temporary suffering he allows in order to refine me for his pleasure is more than worth the incredible, inexpressible pleasure of living with him at the center of my life—forever.

Bottom Line

It really is all about choice. So let's choose to align our choices with him. Let's let every choice reflect our love for him—and our gratitude for what he has done for us. Let's take the "test" and consciously choose *his* way, *his* truth—*his* BEST—in every situation of our lives!

Chapter Summary

Step 8: Choose to Follow God

1. You make choices every day—every moment—to live life your own small and selfish way or God's perfect and lovely way; and all choices have consequences.
2. Your real bottom-line choice is experiencing pure delight in fellowship with God, which has its share of difficulty, or being in bondage to the enemy, which will wreak havoc in the long run.
3. Like with the woman at the well, God offers a real satisfaction that doing things your way cannot.
4. As you practice obedience, your love for God will grow; as your love for God grows, the more willing you are to obey.
5. Putting God ahead of "self" takes commitment and practice—and the help of the Holy Spirit.

Challenge!

1. Awareness leads to choice, and choice can lead to change. What has God been showing you in this chapter about something you may choose to change?

_____

_____

_____

_____

2. Think about a time when you were tempted to do something your way rather than God's way. Which did you choose? What were the consequences? How would the consequences be different if you had made the opposite choice?

_____

_____

_____

_____

3. In the past, have you ever paid a price for doing something you knew was wrong? What did you do? What was the "price"?

_____

_____

_____

_____

4. Has Satan ever fooled you—made something look so attractive or even innocent—so that you fell for his lie? What was that? How do you see it now?

_____

_____

_____

_____

5. Jesus modeled obedience for us when he submitted to his Father's authority. Is there any area in your life you have not yet submitted to him? If so, are you willing to put it into his safekeeping now? If yes, tell him so. If no, explain why not.

_____

_____

_____

_____

6. Doing things God's way sometimes can be painful. Can you think of an example in your own life when you experienced discomfort in order to obey him and his commands? What was the outcome? Do you feel he honored your choice to be obedient? How so?

_____

_____

_____

_____

Involve God in Your Resolve!

God's yoke is easy and his burden is light.

Dear Jesus, thank you for what you did for me on the cross. There is no way I can ever begin to repay you for that. But I can demonstrate my love for you by obedience—by making moment-by-moment choices that honor you. When I'm tempted to rebel and do

*things my own way instead of yours, remind me that
there's a price to pay either way—but disobedience
leads to pain and bondage. Obeying you leads to peace,
joy, and freedom. And I am not alone in my efforts;
your Holy Spirit is in me, helping me to will and to act
according to your good purpose (Philippians 2:12–14).
Best of all, I know that as I daily submit myself to
you, we are growing in our intimacy. You are my true
treasure and my greatest pleasure! I love you, Lord!*

What else do you want to ask God right now? What else do
you want to tell him?

_____

_____

_____

_____

_____

*I pray this in the name of your precious Son, Jesus.
Amen.*

What do you sense he is saying to you right now?

_____

_____

_____

_____

====== Step 9 ======

Create Godly Habits

But I say, walk and live [habitually] in the [Holy] Spirit [responsive to and controlled and guided by the Spirit]; then you will certainly not gratify the cravings and desires of the flesh (of human nature without God).

Galatians 5:16 AMP

Okay. I want to make good choices. I want to get in the habit of putting God's will first, of doing things his way, not mine. So *how* do I do it?

I'm glad you asked!

You remember that, as we talked about our "design," we said this: events trigger feelings and self-talk, and that self-talk plays into the results we get. *But,* the real key is that we have a *choice* in the matter! We can choose to change our self-talk and get different and more beneficial outcomes. As we consistently practice this process—exchanging old thoughts for new and true thoughts—we are creating new, positive habits in both our thinking and our behavior. And TED can help you do just that!

TED[1]

Here is a model based on a simple acronym that really works. I know because I use it AND because other people use it to successfully change unproductive self-talk into productive, encouraging, validating dialogue.

Here's how it works.

You've been praying and asking the Lord to show you where your mind has been ruminating on false information or unhealthy thoughts. One day you're driving to the market and discover yourself saying, "I wish I hadn't committed to that dinner tonight. I feel ugly and boring, and no one is going to want to be around me. I'll end up being excluded or ignored."

*T*ime-Out

*E*xamine

*D*etermine

Have you ever heard the term *self-fulfilling prophecy*? It means that what we say and expect is likely what we'll get. And the internal dialogue above is probably going to result in exactly what it is predicting. That self-talk, if left unchecked, will indeed make you *posture* like you're unattractive and *interact* like you're boring—and the outcome of that approach to the party may very well be that you are overlooked.

So, let's *choose* to change our thinking and apply TED to this scenario.

First, take a **Time-Out**. Disrupt the flow of your thinking. Take a deep breath and change your posture. Sit up straight wherever you are and square your shoulders. Make yourself aware of God's presence with you.

Next, **Examine** the words and attitudes in your self-talk. Are they true? Helpful? Consistent with what God says about you? What might be the likely consequences of these perceptions if you continue to soak them up in your mind?

Challenge your thinking. Are you ugly? No! Even on your worst day. Ephesians 2:10 tells us that we are God's workmanship. Workmanship means "work of art" or "masterpiece." You are his work of art. He created you, and you are beautiful!

Further, "long before he laid down the earth's foundations, he had us in mind, settled on us as the focus of his love" (Ephesians 1:4–5 Message). And he tells us, "Listen, O daughter, consider and give ear. . . . The king is enthralled by your beauty; honor him, for he is your Lord" (Psalm 45:11).

So you can take that "ugly" thought and toss it in the wind!

Is it true that you are boring? The fact that someone invited you to a dinner means that person valued you enough to want you there. You have ideas and opinions and experiences to share. So forget boring!

Now, **Determine** the outcome you desire. Then think about God's truth, the way he sees it, and "rescript" your new self-talk accordingly. Write it down. It might sound something like this:

> Lord, I am your workmanship—your beautiful work of art! You are enthralled by my beauty, and you are God of the Universe! I am the object of your affection. You have given me a bright mind—a mind that reflects your beauty, your truth, and your love. When I allow you to shine through me, people can't help but be drawn to me. This is going to be a delightful evening!

Now, do you think your dinner might turn out just a bit differently than it would have with your old self-talk? Don't you feel the energy in the words? Remember when we talked about the collective power of the sensory experiences? When you invite God into your heart and mind to *paint a new picture* and to *speak new words*—words of truth—and to *create new feelings*, guess what? You begin to believe him!

Remember the Bonus

As we start to transform the lies of the enemy into statements of truth and replace tempting thoughts with words of God's love and faithfulness, we begin to get different results.

And guess what? As our behaviors, attitudes, and feelings begin to change, and as new habits of thought are formed, we will one day realize that we interpret people, situations, and temptations differently than we did before. We are developing the mind of Christ!

Habits

Staying in the place of submission is a challenge. Any time we have to give up *anything*, it is difficult, let alone relinquishing our rights to ourselves. But as they say, practice makes perfect. It's a matter of breaking old destructive habits and building new godly ones. Bad habits are often hard to break. Our old feelings, unexamined and unchecked over time, lead us into unhealthy patterns of thinking and acting. And before we realize it, those *patterns* become *habits*. But as we reframe old patterns and practice them repeatedly, we can create new, healthy habits.

As we reframe old patterns and practice them repeatedly, we can create new, healthy habits.

I want you to take a moment to do a little exercise. Right now. You may have done it before, but that's okay. Humor me.

Fold your arms across your chest. Now look down and notice whether the right or left arm is on top. Now, do it the opposite way, with the other arm on top. Got it?

How does that feel? Awkward? A bit uncomfortable? Unfamiliar? Probably! Did you have to *think* about it? Like many people, you maybe did the "washing machine" thing with your arms before you finally got them where you wanted them.

Now think about this. When I first asked you to fold your arms, the odds are extremely high that you did it without thinking about it and that it felt completely natural when you did it. It's an unconscious, comfortable habit.

But when I asked you to do it a new and different way, two things resulted:

- You had to consciously think about how to do it, and
- It felt strange and unfamiliar, maybe a little uncomfortable.

That is exactly what we experience when we learn to do something new and/or differently—when we set about creating a *new* habit.

The wonderful news is that the more we do it, the less we have to think about it and the more natural it becomes. Repetition is the key. Aristotle, a philosopher of old, said, "We are what we repeatedly do." And it's true.

Let's revisit TED. As we catch ourselves having unproductive or sinful thoughts, we do a Time-Out; we Examine our thinking and hold it up to God's truth; and we Determine to do it God's way with God's help. We reject the old thought and replace it with God's truth. When we do this repeatedly, we begin to create a new habit of thought. Pretty soon it's an automatic response, and we don't even have to think about it.

Some of our habits are so ingrained, we no longer recognize the truth when it hits us in the nose! We have conditioned our minds to see reality in a certain way, and it is very difficult to change.

Elephants and Barracudas

Years ago a university study was done to look at the effects of behavioral conditioning. For their experiment they placed a barracuda in a large fish tank. In case you don't remember, a barracuda is a big, long skinny fish with sharp, jagged teeth protruding in an unseemly manner from the front of its mouth. It is also very fierce and aggressive. And it just loves Spanish mackerel for dinner. The scientists dropped a heavy sheet of clear plate glass in the tank, separating one side of the tank from the other. They then dropped a nice plump Spanish mackerel in the opposite end from the barracuda.

Well, you can imagine the excitement and delight of our large, toothy friend when he saw his next meal! (I don't even *want* to think about what the mackerel was feeling.) He immediately shot across the tank, zooming in for the kill.

BAM! He hit the glass. Dazed and stunned, he circled back around in his side of the tank, and as he made the turn on the far end, he again saw the mackerel and, once more, bolted for his prey.

WHUMP! He hit the glass again. This continued for a while longer. Eventually, he learned to make an abrupt turn just before hitting the partition. He was learning. At last, he simply swam in lazy circles, seeing the juicy mackerel in easy reach but knowing he couldn't get to it.

After he demonstrated that behavior for a while, the scientists removed the glass partition in the tank. And guess what happened? Nothing! The barracuda continued to swim in the same pattern. He had been *conditioned* to believe there was a barrier that prevented him from reaching the mackerel. In spite of the *reality* of now having complete access to his dinner, he firmly believed otherwise. And his beliefs ruled his behavior.

Elephant trainers do the same kind of conditioning. When they begin working with a small, young elephant, they clamp a heavy manacle on one hind leg and use a hefty chain to restrain him. The little guy strains and pulls, testing the limited circumference of his freedom in every way possible. Over time he learns that he cannot move beyond the length of his tether. By the time he is an enormous and powerful adult, he can be restrained with a piece of rope and a stake in the ground!

This same beast who can easily uproot a large tree believes he is limited by the length of the rope, but in truth a small tug would set him free.

Messages

"You're not pretty enough." "You'll never be able to do that." "You're so stupid." "You're a waste of space." These are the ugly words that form the glass partitions in our lives. Actions build false barriers too, and as we know, they speak louder than words. Sometimes the barriers are placed gently and with good intentions. "Sweetheart, maybe you should just settle for a job instead of college." "Lots of girls would be happy to marry him." "Don't set your sights too high—you'll only be disappointed."

If, after hearing these erroneous messages, we adopt them as true, it is very difficult to change our wrong perceptions. We are *conditioned* and no longer capable of seeing reality. That's why we are so dependent on God's Word. As we feed his truth into our minds over and over, the truth begins to come to life. Trusting him, we can take our first steps into the infinite possibilities of our new reality. Gradually, we begin to *realize* and actually *believe* that the old sheet of glass isn't even there.

Initiative

To get access to God's power for growth and change, we must take the initiative. We can't just sit around and wait for him to do something. When Jesus healed a man's shriveled hand, he first said, "Reach out your hand" (Mark 3:5 TLB). The man was required to act first, and then Jesus miraculously and powerfully healed him. When a group of men brought a paralyzed friend to Jesus to be healed, he didn't just touch him and heal him. He said, "I tell you, get up, take your mat and go home" (Mark 2:11). "The remarkable thing about spiritual initiative is that the life and power comes after we 'get up and get going.' God does not give us overcoming life—He gives us life *as we overcome*."[2]

We must take the initiative to do things differently and to believe different things.

It will be more difficult for us to get free of an unwanted sin if we don't make some behavioral changes. If we hang out in the same wrong places and with the same wrong people, change will be difficult. If we wallow in excuses and blame, we won't see much improvement. If we keep going back to the sin, it will continue to hold us in its grasp. We must take the initiative to do things differently and to believe different things. Habits—and habits of thought—can be difficult to break, but with God's help, they can be broken.

Years ago a friend sent me this story. I don't know where she got it, but I have thought about it repeatedly over the years.

I walk down the street. There is a deep hole in the sidewalk. I fall in. I am lost . . . I am hopeless. It isn't my fault. It takes forever to find a way out.

I walk down the same street. There is a deep hole in the sidewalk. I pretend I don't see it. I fall in again. I can't believe I'm in the same place. But it isn't my fault. It still takes a long time to get out.

I walk down the same street. There is a deep hole in the sidewalk. I see it is there. I still fall in . . . it's a habit. My eyes are open. I know where I am. It is MY fault. I get out immediately.

I walk down the same street. There is a deep hole in the sidewalk. I walk around it.

I walk down another street.

In the beginning of our journey toward wholeness we may "flirt" with our old sin. "I'll just *look* at it, but I won't go there," we say. "I'll only do it a *little bit*, and then I'll never do it again," we lie to ourselves. That's why we keep falling in the hole. We cannot succeed in our own strength, no matter how strong or determined we are. "'Not by might nor by power, but by my Spirit,' says the LORD Almighty" (Zechariah 4:6). We won't win over the lies simply "because we think we can do anything of lasting value by ourselves. Our only power and success comes from God" (2 Corinthians 3:5 TLB). As we lean on him, he'll teach us to walk down a different street.

The Routing of The Beast

You may be wondering why I came up with the label "The Beast" for my struggle. First of all, it needed a short, descriptive name, because in the course of conversations with my counselor, it was unwieldy to constantly be referring to "this huge collection of overwhelming and horrible thoughts, feelings, temptations, and emotions" in every other sentence. Second, it *felt* like a "thing," even though it was simply a stronghold—evidence of Satan's power over me with this particular struggle. And third, if you haven't guessed by now, I think in pictures, and the composite of my sensory experiences with this "thing" looked and felt to me like a gargantuan, ugly, slimy, evil, grotesque beast. Hence, The Beast.

Because I willingly fed it for years, it was big and strong and robust. It started as a seedling habit, leafed into an obsession, and bloomed into an addiction. In my mind's eye—once I saw it for what it was—its black, rotten, slimy tendrils snaked their way deep down into, around, and throughout my heart, like a large shrub entangles its roots with the roots of a tree.

I lived with it for so long that it became comfortable and familiar. I turned to it when I was hurting. It took me to a fantasy land where love, happiness, contentment, excitement, and dreams seemed so very real. It had control and it was powerful.

Then came the awakening—the day God showed me what it really looked like. I was appalled. I knew it had to go. And I knew it had to be ripped out—by the roots. The battle ensued.

I won't lie to you. It wasn't easy. It was a full-blown war, and I lost many of the skirmishes. It hurt. Especially the pulling-it-out-by-the-roots part. As I cried out to God to take it, my hands went through the motions of ripping it away from my chest. I could see and feel the bleeding, hurting, gaping hole left behind.

I soon learned it wasn't enough to rip it out; an empty hole begs to be filled. And The Beast was always more than willing to come back. So I learned to fill it with God's healing love. I pictured him pouring his warm, soothing liquid love into the gap. It filled and overflowed the wounded, gaping cavity and trickled into all the little hurting places of my heart.

Do you have a "beastly" habit? Are you ready to be free of it?

I repeated this process many times. But as days and months passed by, something happened. I noticed I was stronger. The battles were less frequent. The relapses rarer. I noticed actual progress. I knew the enemy was still lurking out there, but I was using all of God's armor to keep him at bay. I had an excellent Christian counselor who challenged my old, untrue beliefs and immersed me in God's Word. I had friends who prayed for me and encouraged me. At last, I reached a point where the battle gradually subsided.

I now had some new, successful habits in place, both in my thinking and in my behaviors.

I know not to venture anywhere near those old habits and traps that "set me off." I know The Beast is still out there, but it is under God's control as long as I partner with him to control it. That doesn't mean it won't make forays into my life just to check my defenses.

Each time it does, I lay everything before God, pray for his strength, and thank him for his help in advance. And He is faithful. "Oh, praise the Lord, for he has listened to my pleadings! He is my strength, my shield from every danger. I trusted in him, and he helped me. Joy rises in my heart until I burst out in songs of praise to him" (Psalm 28:6–7 TLB).

Do you have a "beastly" habit? What is it? Are you ready to be free of it?

Chapter Summary

Step 9: Create Godly Habits

1. It's important to recognize and deal with old, untrue beliefs you may have about yourself, your value, your loveliness.
2. New habits require conscious thought and effort, and will feel unfamiliar and awkward in the beginning. But every time you repeat them, you're getting closer to making them new, better habits.
3. Practicing new habits and habits of thought over time will result in new habits that are comfortable and almost automatic.
4. You need to take the initiative.

Challenge!

One way we begin to break away from negative and nonproductive self-talk is to reframe our thoughts. On the worksheet that follows, use the TED model to change an untrue belief or thought you have from time to time.

Exercise: Self-Talk

We all chatter nonstop with ourselves. Some of what we say is positive and helpful; some is not. It's important to be aware of the negative messages that romp through our minds, because with repetition, we will internalize them as true, whether or not they are.

Instructions

Think of some of the negative things you say to yourself. Write down two or three.

(Examples: I'm so *stupid* • I'll *never* get this done • She's going to *hate* me for this • I'm *always* late • I have the *worst* hair • *Nothing* looks good on me • Sometimes I just *hate* myself • I don't *deserve* to be loved)

- _____

- _____

- _____

Now, pick just one of them for this exercise. Got it? Good!

Next, walk through the completed TED model so you'll get the idea of how this works. We're using a simple example. Feel free to skip ahead and do the blank one on your own!

Sample

Applying the TED Model

Write out your negative or nonproductive self-talk statement here:

I don't deserve to be loved!

Time-Out. Interrupt the flow of your thinking. *Done*
- Take a deep breath and change your posture. *Done*
- Sit up straight and square your shoulders. *Done*
- Make yourself aware of God's presence with you. *Focusing . . .*
- Invite him to explore your thoughts with you. *Done*

Examine the words and attitudes in your self-talk.
- Are they encouraging? Helpful? *Not really*
- Challenge your thinking. Is it true? *Maybe. I'm not sure. I don't feel deserving right now.*
- Is it consistent with God's truth? *I have to say no. His word says I have great value.*
- What might be the likely consequences of these perceptions if you continue to soak them up in your mind? *I'll continue to feel bad about myself—or feel even worse. And I'll be believing something that God says isn't true.*

Determine the outcome *you* desire. Frame new helpful, true self-talk.
- What is my desired outcome in this situation? *I want to feel loved! Lovable! Worthy of love!*

- Look at it from the perspective of God's truth. Write down how you're choosing to look at it now—based on that truth.

  God, you tell me that you love me. In fact, I know your Son died for me. I choose to believe your truth in my life. I'm deserving of your love because of Jesus. And if you love me, nothing else really matters. (And I do know that others love me too.)

- Create your new self-talk based on God's truth; write it down.

  Because Jesus died for me, I have incredible worth and I am completely deserving of God's incredible love!

- Close your eyes for a moment. In your mind, you're going to paint a vivid picture of this new outcome.

  First, what does this new outcome *look* like for you. Can you see it?

  Next, attach the new, wonderful feelings you have to the picture. Can you *feel* them?

  Repeat your new, true self-talk words. Can you *hear* them?

  Now, add bright colors, joyful sounds, pleasant aromas, and any other enjoyable sensory images you like to your picture. Can you *see* and *sense* them?

  Finally, invite Jesus into your picture. *See him* smiling at you and *be aware of* the way he's looking at you with adoration. Is he holding your hand? Sitting next to you? Hugging you? Create the picture you want.

  Now, simply *savor the entire picture* in your mind in as much detail as you can.

- Thank God for his love and guidance. Ask him to make you aware of the next time you tell yourself the old lie, and to remind you to replace it with God's new truth.

Applying the TED Model

Write out your negative or nonproductive self-talk statement here:

Time-Out. Interrupt the flow of your thinking.
- Take a deep breath and change your posture.
- Sit up straight and square your shoulders.
- Make yourself aware of God's presence with you.
- Invite him to explore your thoughts with you.

Examine the words and attitudes in your self-talk.
- Are they encouraging? Helpful?

_____

_____

- Challenge your thinking. Is it true?

_____

_____

_____

- Is it consistent with God's truth?

_____

_____

_____

- What might be the likely consequences of these perceptions if you continue to soak them up in your mind?

_____

_____

_____

Determine the outcome *you* desire. Frame new helpful, true self-talk.
- What is my desired outcome in this situation?

_____

_____

_____

- Look at it from the perspective of God's truth. Write down how you're choosing to look at it now—based on that truth.

_____

_____

_____

_____

- Create your new self-talk based on God's truth; write it down.

_____

_____

_____

_____

- Close your eyes for a moment. In your mind, you're going to paint a vivid picture of this new outcome.

    First, what does this new outcome *look* like for you. Can you see it?

    Next, attach the new, wonderful feelings you have to the picture. Can you *feel* them?

    Repeat your new, true self-talk words. Can you *hear* them?

    Now, add bright colors, joyful sounds, pleasant aromas, and any other enjoyable sensory images you like to your picture. Can you *see* and *sense* them?

    Finally, invite Jesus into your picture. *See him* smiling at you and *be aware of* the way he's looking at you with adoration. Is he holding your hand? Sitting next to you? Hugging you? Create the picture you want.

    Now, simply *savor the entire picture* in your mind in as much detail as you can.

- Thank God for his love and guidance. Ask him to make you aware of the next time you tell yourself the old lie, and to remind you to replace it with God's new truth.

Involve God in Your Resolve!

God sees what you already are—and what you can become as you trust and obey him.

> *Dearest Father, you know everything about me, including the lies and limitations I sometimes believe about myself. And I know you see the freedom I will have as I relinquish false belief and embrace your truth. Father, show me the error of my thinking. Reveal to me the habits, and habits of thought, that keep me from walking your perfect path and from being all you intend me to be. I want everything I believe to be consistent with your Word and your promises. Walk with me as I choose to make necessary changes. Help me to "be constantly renewed in the spirit of [my] mind, [having a fresh mental and spiritual attitude]" (Ephesians 4:22–24 AMP). I thank you that you are providing me with the knowledge, strength, and wisdom to change my old, ingrained beliefs and to create new, true ways of thinking. I love that you tell me I am your beautiful masterpiece, your work of art! And because of what you did for me, I also have great value and worth. I will incorporate those truths into all my beliefs. As a result, my words and actions will glorify you! I thank you, Lord, that at any time I can come to you and drink from your well of boundless, life-restoring, fresh spring water!*

What else do you want to ask God right now? What else do you want to tell him?

_____

_____

_____

_____

_____

I pray this in your precious name, Jesus. Amen.

What do you sense he is saying to you right now?

_____

_____

_____

_____

Part III

Our Victory!

$$===== \text{Step } 10 =====$$

Trust God for All Your Needs

And my God will liberally supply (fill to the full) your every
need according to His riches in glory in Christ Jesus.

Philippians 4:19 AMP

The king was conducting business before his throne. Everyone
in the castle, even his wife, knew that it was forbidden to
interrupt him while he was working. After all, he was the
king. He commanded legions of soldiers and created law
for the entire domain. His name was legendary. Young men
spoke it with awe; old men, with reverence.

He sat before the leaders of state, a pensive expression on his
face as he studied the documents in his lap. Suddenly the door
to the room burst open, startling the dignitaries gathered in the
room. The patter of little feet could be heard running across
the hard stone floor, directly toward the king on his throne.
The small assembly audibly gasped, stunned at the intrusion
and not knowing what the king's reaction would be.

"Daddy, Daddy! I found a yellow flower!" It was the king's
small daughter.

In a single motion the king swept the little girl off her
feet and into his lap, scattering the important papers to the

floor. His preoccupied countenance immediately transformed into sheer delight as he smiled broadly at his child and then examined her small prize. While the luminaries waited, she sat there with him, her tiny form cuddled in the crook of his strong and gentle right arm. With her head pressed against his chest, they shared secrets and some small talk. He made her giggle, and then, after kisses and a big hug, the little girl, smiling from ear to ear and glowing with contentment, climbed down from her daddy's lap and ran out of the room.

Our Daddy

That's what our Daddy is like. He is King of the universe, but we can run to him and jump in his lap anytime we want to. He is never too busy, and he is always overjoyed to be with us, his little girls. He is fully interested in our lives and is there to meet even our smallest needs. Why? Because he loves us.

Think about it. Why was Jesus willing to step down from his magnificent throne in heaven and subject himself to the ugliness of the world? He was fully God and fully man, but he chose to be stripped of his wondrous, almighty godhood to become a helpless baby and, later on, a maligned man. And why did he consent to go through his excruciating ordeal on the cross?

Love. Amazing, perfect love. For us. Sinful, imperfect us.

He died solely so we can have a loving, intimate relationship with him. God. Almighty Creator. Because he loves us and desires our love in return. He created us for his *pleasure*. We belong to him.

Trusting His Purpose

God allows everything in our lives for a purpose. His purpose. A higher purpose. When we begin with the assumption that he has only the best intentions for us, we then have the foundation for trusting him. Think about it. He loves us and has loved us from the beginning of time. Because our sin separated us from an intimate relationship with him, he sent his Son to earth to die for us. Jesus could have prevented his own painful death. He could have called on a thousand angels to save him from the horrors of his torture and his crucifixion. But he didn't. He made a choice. In the midst of excruciating pain he chose his Father's HIGH way instead of HIS way. He chose to endure the suffering so we could enjoy sweet fellowship with him. Here on earth and forever. What a sacrificial gift!

He wants us to know beyond a doubt that we are beautiful, cherished, valued, and deeply loved by him.

That is love. "Not that we loved God, but that he loved us and sent his Son as an atoning sacrifice for our sins" (1 John 4:10). He shows us his love in his Word. The apostle John tells us, "How great is the love the Father has lavished on us, that we should be called children of God!" (1 John 3:1).

And because he loves us so much, he wants to meet our deepest needs. He wants us to know beyond a doubt that we are beautiful, cherished, valued, and deeply loved by him.

You Are Beautiful . . .

The fashion world sets our standard for beauty, and most of us buy into it. As a result we are constantly trying to change ourselves to fit the ideal. The strange thing is, the ideal changes over time. Think back to the old portraits painted several hundred years ago. The "beautiful" women were, shall we say, curvy and quite ample! Jump forward in time and notice that even in Marilyn Monroe's era women had hips and, well, meat on their bones. Quite a contrast to today's models, who look to be 5′10″ and 95 pounds.

Short or tall, chunky or skinny, perfect or imperfect, we need to remember that God created us as his work of art. The psalmist says, "You made all the delicate, inner parts of my body, and knit them together in my mother's womb . . . It is amazing to think about. Your workmanship is marvelous" (Psalm 139:13–14 TLB). No matter what we look like by society's standards, we are beautiful in God's eyes. He loves variety, as evidenced in all of his creation. And while the world's standards continually change, his do not. He made each of us pleasing to himself. So next time you don't feel like you measure up, look yourself in the eye in the mirror and say to God—with a smile and with conviction—"YOU think I'm beautiful!" And it's absolutely true.

You Are Valued . . .

Do you realize that if you were the only person in the world, Jesus would have died just for you? What does that say about your value? Let's go back to Psalm 139 again and see what else the psalmist has to say. "How precious it is, Lord, to realize that you are thinking about me constantly! I can't even count how many times a day your thoughts turn towards me. And when I waken in the morning, you are still thinking of me!" (vv. 17–18 TLB). If the Lord of the universe thinks about you constantly, you must be incredibly special.

You have great worth and value to God. No matter what has happened in your life, no matter how many mistakes you have made. Nothing changes your worth. Our pastor demonstrated this concept in a creative way. He held up a crisp, new twenty-dollar bill and asked people in the front row, "Do any of you want this?" Hands flew up with enthusiasm, and a couple of people jumped to their feet with outstretched palms. He said, "First, let me do this," and he proceeded to crumple up the money into a tight wad in his fist. He smoothed out the wrinkled bill and queried his audience, "Do you still want it?" Enthusiasm again erupted in the front row. "But wait," he said, "what if I do this?" Throwing the bill down, he ground it into the floor with his heel. He picked it up, now all wrinkled and dirty, and held it in the air. "Now who wants it?" No surprise, people still clamored for the twenty-dollar bill.

Had the value of the bill changed? Of course it hadn't. Not even with misuse.

It's the same in our lives. No matter how "rumpled" or "dirty" we are, our value to God never changes. And he makes all things new. He values us so highly that by his grace he gives us a fresh start—over and over again.

You Are Cherished . . .

Just as the king cherished his little girl, God cherishes you. He loves you and values you. He defends you and protects you. Because he adores you. He wants to be with you—even more than you want to be with him.

Listen to this: "You are a daughter of the King, and not just any king. You are *My* daughter, and I am the God of all heaven and earth. *I'm delighted with you!* You are the apple of My eye. You're Daddy's girl. . . . I formed your body. I fashioned your mind and soul. I know your personality, and I understand your needs and desires. . . . I love you passionately and patiently. . . . know that—although I am God—my arms are not too big to hold you, My beloved daughter."[1]

Can you feel it? Do you understand how much he cherishes you? I hope so!

You Are Deeply Loved . . .

One of my favorite pieces of Scripture is Ephesians 3:17–19 in the Living Bible:

167

May your roots go down deep into the soil of God's marvelous love; and may you be able to feel and understand, as all God's children should, how long, how wide, how deep, and how high his love really is; and to experience this love for yourselves, though it is so great that you will never see the end of it or fully know or understand it. And so at last you will be filled up with God himself.

Isn't that a beautiful picture? And it can only *attempt* to show us the extent of God's love.

I once heard a pastor describe the impossibility of communicating God's unfathomable expanse of love for us. In his story, you meet someone who has never seen the ocean, or even pictures of the ocean. In your effort to explain it to him, you show him a big jug of seawater and then try to describe how gargantuan the ocean really is. Obviously, he can see the water in the container. He can even touch it and taste it. But he won't be able to grasp the magnitude of the ocean. He sees only a teeny part and must try to imagine the rest based on the picture you describe.

The more we learn to trust in him and obey him, the more of his love we see.

I'm convinced that God's love is much the same and just as indescribable. The more we learn to trust in him and obey him, the more of his love we see. But as mere humans we cannot begin to comprehend the unending expansiveness of his love. It is beyond our ability to imagine. For now, "We can see and understand only a little about God . . . as if we were peering at his reflection in a poor mirror; but someday we are going to see him in his completeness, face to face" (1 Corinthians 13:12 TLB). And because "God *IS* love" (1 John 4:16, emphasis mine), I suspect that when we get to heaven and see him for the first time, the sheer "weight" of his love will bowl us over!

Imagine. God Almighty—Creator of the vast universe and Designer of the microscopic wonders of our world—loves us.

He loves you. He loves me. And he loves us with a love that is so vast it is outside the realm of our knowledge. Wow.

When he looks at you, he sees the object of his intense desire. The fruition of his unique design. The little girl he calls "my beautiful daughter"! When we allow him to gaze for a moment into our eyes, we see a love we've never known—never will know, apart from him. We are cherished. We are valued. We are adored. He sees all of our flaws and blemishes, and loves us passionately anyway. He wants to laugh with us in our hilarity and cry with us in our distress. He wants to hold our hand when we need a loving, caring, and constant companion. He wants to dance with us and frolic with us. And when we just need to be held, he wants to embrace us in his incredibly strong, warm, loving arms.

Integrating God's Truth

This is God's truth. Do you believe it? I hope so! But more important, if you *believe* it, do you *think* and *act* like you believe it? Does your behavior reflect the fact that you are loved perfectly by a perfect God? Do your thoughts and attitudes validate the fact that you are a daughter of the King, with a value far greater than a king's ransom?

As you begin to believe and integrate his truth about you, you begin to experience the reality of it. You walk differently—with chin up and head held high, and maybe a little bounce in your step. You talk differently—with self-assurance (make that "God-assurance"), gentleness, and authority. And you think differently—with a focus on others and on God rather than self, with great awe at what God has done and continues to do for you. You have a growing, deep-down confidence as well as feelings of great worth in Jesus—and nothing else can shake that. You realize that he values you above rubies and diamonds and proved that by giving his life for you. And in the end, you see that he is the answer to all your needs—for feeling loved, cherished, adored, and valued.

Chapter Summary

Step 10: Trust God for All Your Needs

1. God *loves* you, more deeply and completely than you can imagine.
2. *Everything* has a purpose in his perfect plan for your life.
3. He knows you intimately, and you can trust him with your every need.
4. In his eyes you are beautiful, have great value, and are worth being cherished.
5. The more you trust and obey him, the more of his love you'll be able to see.

Challenge!

1. Are you comfortable believing that God loves you— deeply and completely—like his cherished daughter? Did any particular verses or descriptions make it easier for you to accept this fact? If so, how might you use them as a reminder to you throughout your day?

_____

_____

_____

2. Is it more important to you to be beautiful by the world's standards or in God's eyes? Explain your answer.

_____

_____

_____

_____

3. In the world, you may sometimes feel that you are not beautiful, or you may believe you are not truly loved and cherished. How can you incorporate God's truth about your loveliness and value *to him* into your thinking? How will that change your life for the better?

_____

_____

_____

_____

4. Does it help you to know that as you seek to love and obey him, you can trust him with your *every* need? Are you willing to tell him about each of your longings and unmet needs, and then to trust him to fulfill your desires in his way?

_____

_____

_____

_____

Involve God in Your Resolve!

God loves you beyond your wildest imaginings. You can trust him with every single one of your needs.

As you conclude this chapter, I invite you to stop for a moment and pray in your own words. Begin by telling God what his love means to you. Share your heart with him. You are his precious daughter—he wants to hear about your thoughts, dreams, and desires. Tell him about them. He wants to walk and talk with you. And he desires for you to learn to abide with him. As you linger at his side, you will discover comfort and pleasure in his presence. As you dwell with him, tell him what it is you really need, and in time, you'll find he is all you ever needed—and more.

What do you sense he is saying to you right now?

_____

_____

_____

_____

Make an Honest Evaluation

The thief comes only to steal and kill and destroy; I have come that they may have life, and have it to the full.

Jesus

Abundance. That's what Jesus offers. Not just life, but life *to the full*. Not mediocrity, but *excellence*. Not just circumstantial happiness, but *deep-down, all-pervasive joy!*

God's path is so much easier and his blessings are so far beyond any joys the world has to offer that there is no comparison. Choosing to sin keeps us from his "easy yoke" and harnesses us to a cruel and uncaring master who only wants to steal, kill, and destroy. When we focus on ourselves, we miss freedom and abundant living.

The Luxury Cruise

Let's take a hypothetical vacation. Imagine yourself and your best friend (we'll call her Elaine) on the first day of a long-awaited luxury cruise to Hawaii. As the ship pulls away from the dock, you look at each other with big grins and then break into singsong voices, "We're going to Hawaii! We're going to Hawaii!" (Maybe you and your friends are way too sophisticated for that sort of thing, but my friends and I aren't.)

After the muster drill and unpacking suitcases, you go your separate ways but agree to meet for dinner. You head to the gym and pool to check out fitness programs while Elaine explores the spa and the climbing wall everyone's been talking about.

The dinner hour arrives and you head for the main dining area. No sign of Elaine yet. When the doors open, you decide to wait inside at your table. Informal introductions are made all around, and with the typical conversational chitchat that ensues, you explain the absence of your friend the best you can. Dinner arrives and still no Elaine. Hmmm . . . that's odd, but she's a big girl and will show up when she pleases.

You check out the menu. Wow! What a feast! Your sophisticated European waiter assures you and your new companions that you can have as much of anything you want *and* informs you of what else is available, even though not on the menu. Hog heaven!

"Let's see . . . ," you say to yourself, "think I'll start with that yummy shrimp cocktail François recommends." (That's "frahn-swah," in case you don't speak French.) "He said the shrimp are *huge*! And then . . . perhaps the romaine salad with sugar-roasted almonds and mandarin oranges, served with a sweet sesame-seed dressing. And for the main dish . . . hmmm . . . it's so hard to choose. Do I want the pork medallions with apricot sauce, the crusted ahi served with papaya relish, or the Hawaiian coconut chicken with pineapple, sweet peppers, and water chestnuts? But, of course, there's also the Maine lobster with drawn garlic butter!"

By the time you top off your immense meal with fresh-brewed coffee, an individually prepared lemon soufflé, and "just a small scoop of French vanilla ice cream with mint chocolate sauce, please," you can hardly waddle back to your stateroom.

As you walk in the door, you find your roommate sitting on the edge of her bed just finishing up *her* dinner—a PBJ sandwich and an apple!

As it turns out, Elaine has packed a week's worth of food for the journey to Hawaii. She had no idea gourmet meals were included with the cruise. (I told you this was a hypothetical trip—EVERY woman knows a cruise is all about the food!)

The point is this: accepting Christ as your Savior—but then refusing to let him be Lord and Master of your life—is like going on a luxury cruise and packing your own brown-bag lunch. You've got the "ticket to heaven" and you're on your way, but instead of feasting at the banquet table during the journey, you are settling for junk food.

Instead of feasting at the banquet table during the journey, you are settling for junk food.

So, where are you taking your meals? Are you joyously laughing and celebrating at the Captain's table, relishing the cruise of a lifetime? Or are you holed up alone in a dark and dismal storage closet, eating from a rumpled brown bag and behaving like an unworthy stowaway?

Taking Stock—Where Are You?

No one but you and the Lord know where you stand in your Christian walk. If you're like me, you sometimes feel you're moving forward; at other times, backward. The important thing is your heart. If your heart is set on God, the forward-backward movement isn't all that important—you *will* make progress. But if you're not really sure you want to make a complete commitment to living for the Lord, you're in danger of regressing more than progressing.

Decision Time

We've come to the point where it's time to do an assessment. Who or what are you trusting in your life right now to fulfill your need for love and fulfillment? Are you eating at the table of the world or at the table of God's abundant love?

As you do the work with the exercises that follow, I want to encourage you to be candid with yourself. Invite God to accompany you with each task. Ask him to make the cloudy areas clear and the hidden things plain.

Exercise #1: The Ideal Man

How would you rate your level of commitment to God *right now*? Think about your *present* willingness to give up the things he might want you to give up, your willingness to put his desires ahead of your own, your willingness to make changes in the way you are presently living your life. What is your level of commitment? Be honest.

Not Very Committed	Somewhat Committed	Pretty Much Committed	Very Committed	Completely Committed
1	2	3	4	5

Take a moment to imagine an "ideal man." Go ahead, forget reality! Think about the qualities and characteristics he would have. Then in your own words, provide a specific and detailed description for each of the questions below. For the "ideal man" in question, spend some time thinking about and describing how he would

- relate to you, connect with you

  _____

  _____

- act with you, treat you

  _____

  _____

- feel about being with you and spending time with you

  _____

  _____

- speak to you, communicate with you

_____

_____

- make you feel

_____

_____

Remember, these are *your* opinions only—not what you believe someone else would think. Now, answer the following:

A. What would the *absolutely ideal* **father** look like to you?

- From your perspective as a little girl:

_____

_____

- From your perspective as an adolescent girl:

_____

_____

- From your perspective as an adult woman:

_____

_____

B. What would the *absolutely ideal* **husband** look like to you?

_____

_____

_____

C. What would the *absolutely ideal* **brother** look like to you?

_____

_____

_____

D. What would the *absolutely ideal* **guy friend** look like to you?

_____

_____

_____

If your descriptions include traits that are godly, loving, caring, gentle, kind, honorable, encouraging, supportive, happy, fun, delightful, wise, and fair, you've just described your "ideal man"—your perfect heavenly Father. But he is so much MORE!

PART III

Think about the "ideal man" you just described. God is all that and more. As you picture God that way, how would you describe your *ideal relationship* with him? Write down your thoughts.

A. Describe how you *feel* about him. What you *think* of him.

_____

_____

_____

B. In light of all he gives to you, what are you willing to do for him? What are you willing to give up for him?

_____

_____

_____

C. NOW—in this "ideal" relationship, and in light of this complete love he has for you, what is your level of commitment to him?

Not Very Committed	Somewhat Committed	Pretty Much Committed	Very Committed	Completely Committed
1	2	3	4	5

D. Has your commitment level changed? If so, how? If not, why?

_____

_____

_____

ACTION

What are you willing to do right now to live your life with more complete commitment to him?

_____

_____

_____

Exercise #2: Invisible Barriers

Struggles with issues from the past are common. Few of us have come through life unscathed. It may be that we were mistreated with words, or attitudes, or worse. If we interpreted those bad experiences incorrectly—as most of us did—it becomes confusing and problematic as we now try to redefine ourselves in light of God's truth about us. Those old, incorrect convictions create limiting beliefs or artificial barriers, like with the barracuda, about who we are and who we can be.

I often hear well-intentioned people quote Philippians 3:13–14: "But one thing I do: *Forgetting what is behind* [emphasis mine] and straining toward what is ahead, I press on toward the goal." They will tell you to "forget the ugliness of the past and get on with it!" But before "moving on," it is important to *deal* with the old wounds rather than bury them. Otherwise it's like slapping disinfectant and a Band-Aid on a badly infected wound. It may provide some instant relief and fool you into believing it's "all better," but in time the swelling, festering, and agony return, and you must rip off the dirty bandage and begin the process again.

The process of "cleaning out the wound" by digging out all the infection may be painful, but it's amazing the complete relief you experience once it heals properly. We *do* need to "press on" or, in other words, stop just thinking about it and take action. If you do not see progress in healing your past, don't hesitate to seek the help of a qualified pastor or Christian counselor.

We often let artificial barriers and incorrect beliefs prevent us from seeing ourselves as God sees us and from believing we can become all God intends us to be. This exercise is designed to help you look at some of the incorrect beliefs you may have about yourself.

Instructions

Read the statement and examples below, then write out as many limiting beliefs as you can. Don't overthink or over-analyze; just note your thoughts and list as many as you can.

A. A belief I allow to stand in the way of feeling completely valued, loved, worthy, beautiful, and/or cherished is:

> **Examples:** I'm not worthy of being loved/good enough to be loved • The *right* man would make me feel loved • Dad was right—I'm ugly/fat/pathetic • If only my husband would change • A really great guy would never be interested in me • I'm such a mess—I can't do anything right • If only . . .

Limiting Beliefs	New Beliefs

B. Read and think about the following:
- "I have great worth apart from my performance because Christ gave his life for me, and therefore, imparted great value to me. I am deeply loved, fully pleasing, totally forgiven, accepted, and complete in Christ."[1]

- Jesus loves me even as the Father loves me. I will live within his love. (John 15:9 TLB)
- Moreover, because of what Christ has done I have become a gift to God that he delights in, for as part of God's sovereign plan I was chosen from the beginning to be his. (Ephesians 1:11 TLB)
- For God so loved me that he gave his only Son. (John 3:16 TLB)
- For I am convinced that nothing can ever separate me from God's love. Death can't, and life can't. The angels won't, and all the powers of hell itself cannot keep God's love away. (Romans 8:38)
- I see how very much you, my heavenly Father, love me, for you allow me to be called your child—think of it—and I really am! (1 John 3:1 TLB)
- And I pray that you, Christ, will be more and more at home in my heart, living within me as I learn to trust in you. Grow my roots down deep into the soil of your marvelous love; and help me to feel and understand, as all God's children should, how long, how wide, how deep, and how high your love really is; and to experience this love for myself, though it is *so great* that I will never fully see the end of it or fully understand it. And so at last I will be filled up with you! (Ephesians 3:17–19 TLB)

C. Now go back and reread your list of limiting beliefs. This time try *God's* point of view! Write down next to each limiting belief a **new belief** you can use to replace it. This is one way to begin overcoming the old lies and replacing them with God's truth.

Jot down two new *true* beliefs you want to focus on over the next few weeks. Reference a supporting Scripture.

FIRST *NEW TRUE* BELIEF

God's *truth* about me—and him—in Scripture:

_____

_____

_____

_____

SECOND *NEW TRUE* BELIEF

God's *truth* about me—and him—in Scripture:

_____

_____

_____

_____

Reaffirm these new beliefs by praying about them each day.

Just Checking . . .

How are you doing? What is God showing you? If what you're seeing seems overwhelming, that's okay. That's God's way of helping us rely on him and his strength! Trust him: you're not doing this alone.

Exercise #3: Obstacles to Fullfilment

Anything we allow to come between us and God is an obstacle to our complete fulfillment. When we allow substitutions, distractions, or avoidance to take the place of his genuine love and care, we rob ourselves of *real* joy.

In chapter 4 we talked about the traps we fall into as we attempt to fill our needs for love and affection. As you read that chapter, you may have identified with some of them. Perhaps it was something you struggled with previously and have now overcome. If so, then praise God! Maybe you read something you're feeling guilty about right now, whether or not it was covered in the discussion. Perhaps you began to think about—maybe question—some of the things you do that seem okay, but now you wonder. Or maybe you're on the brink, about to delve into something that might not be God's *best* for you. But seeing it in black and white causes you to pause.

In the following exercise, I want to encourage you to be brutally honest with yourself. If you are presently struggling with a trap, it may be a difficult process for you. We sometimes rationalize or deny the truth in our own minds, but nothing is hidden from God. As you go through the list, invite God to process each item with you. You can pray, *Lord, help me to be honest with myself. Please show me anything I'm doing that is taking the place of your best for my life. And if there is anything that on the surface seems okay to me but really isn't, please open my eyes to see it the way you see it. Thank you, Lord.*

Instructions

A. Read through this list of behaviors. Make a check next to any that apply to you, or note it in your private journal. This is just between you and the Lord.

Behaviors I engage in or thoughts I think about:

(N = Never; S = Seldom; O = Occasionally; or F = Frequently)

_____ Reading "romance" novels

_____ Reading books that contain fairly graphic sexual descriptions

_____ Buying a magazine because it has something on the cover about sex or romance

_____ Looking at pornographic materials

_____ Watching soap operas

_____ Continuing to watch TV shows or movies when they lead to sexual scenes

_____ Watching TV shows well known for their sexual innuendos or content

_____ Watching movies that have racy content

_____ Watching X-rated movies

_____ Toying with romantic ideas about myself and someone else (if married, not my husband)

_____ Creating detailed mental scenarios about someone loving me or being attracted to me

_____ Fantasizing about being romantically involved with someone, either a fictional character, a celebrity, or someone I actually know

_____ Acting out a romantic interlude, using my pillow, teddy bear, etc.

_____ Toying with thoughts of homosexuality

_____ Using self-gratification (masturbation) as a means of fulfilling a sexual need

_____ Engaging in homosexual activity

_____ If single, engaging in sexual activity (including touching or oral sex)

_____ If married, engaging in extramarital sexual activity

_____ While married, flirting with men other than my husband

_____ While married or unmarried, creating opportunities to "appropriately" touch, hug, or kiss other men, but with the motive being to fulfill an underlying need

_____ While married, creating excuses to spend time with a man to whom I'm attracted

_____ Communicating with men one-on-one in Internet chat rooms

Anything else you're sensing you need to examine?

_____

_____

_____

Remember, this exercise isn't about racking up marks to prove to yourself how "bad" or "sinful" you are. It is simply a method to identify the things that cause you to struggle and prevent you from experiencing all of God's love and joy.

   B. Take another moment to look closely at each of the items you marked as S, O, or F. Ask yourself these questions to determine how deeply you are involved in the behavior:

   - Is this behavior just an occasional distraction?
   - Do I feel frequently and sometimes strongly drawn to it?
   - Do I feel fervently compelled to engage in it, even to the point of missing out on other good or important things in life?

This may make clear how much of a hold this behavior has on you. Again, it's important that you're honest. It's easy to *say*, "I can give it up any time I want," but actually *doing* it is another matter!

   C. Now, look again at each item. Dig deep. Ask God to show you what *real needs* the ineffective behavior is trying to meet. What is the true feeling underneath it? Ask yourself these questions:

   - Am I using this behavior to avoid feelings? What feelings?

- Am I using this behavior as a distraction from a feeling I need to face? What feeling?
- Am I using this behavior as a substitution, to feel something I really want to feel? What are those feelings?

None of these futile behaviors or habits of thought will bring lasting joy. They are counterfeits for the real thing. So, knowing that, what do you want to do? Are you content to let this behavior (or behaviors) keep you from genuine satisfaction and contentment and from honoring God? Or is your heart yearning to feel truly loved and cherished? Will you choose to let go of whatever is keeping you from that?

D. Read and meditate on the following Scriptures:

- Finally, whatever is true, whatever is noble, whatever is right, whatever is pure, whatever is lovely, whatever is admirable—if anything is excellent or praiseworthy—I will think about such things. (Philippians 4:8)
- Since, then, I have been raised with Christ, I will set my heart on things above, where Christ is seated at the right hand of God. I will set my mind on things above, not on earthly things. For I died and my life is now hidden with Christ in God. (Colossians 3:1–3)
- So I will give my body to God. I will let it be a living sacrifice, holy—the kind he can accept. When I think of what he has done for me, is this too much to ask? I won't copy the behavior and customs of this world, but I will be a new and different person with a fresh newness in all I do and think. Then I will learn from my own experience how his ways will really satisfy me. (Romans 12:1–2 TLB)

What are you now feeling about your trap, or maybe your list of traps? What is God asking you to examine? To change? What are you willing to do right now?

_____

_____

_____

_____

As we choose to renounce and repent of our sin, "he is faithful and just and will forgive us our sins and purify us from all unrighteousness" (1 John 1:9). That is the beginning of the healing process!

Exercise #4: Habits

Changing old habits and developing new ones is a challenging process. Remember the arm-crossing exercise we did? In order to do anything in a new and different way, we have to consciously think about it. And for a while it will feel strange and a bit uncomfortable. But the more we do it, the more natural and automatic it will become.

The apostle Peter describes to us the ways in which our faith should continue to grow—in other words, the habits we need to develop as we grow in Christ. "Make every effort to add to your faith goodness; and to goodness, knowledge; and to knowledge, self-control; and to self-control, perseverance; and to perseverance, godliness; and to godliness, brotherly kindness; and to brotherly kindness, love. For if you possess these qualities in increasing measure, they will keep you from being ineffective and unproductive in your knowledge of our Lord Jesus Christ" (2 Peter 1:5–8).

That's a tall order! But it demonstrates the necessity of action in order to develop our faith. These character traits don't just happen—we must work at them until they become habitual attitudes and behaviors. Oswald Chambers puts it this way: "No one is born either naturally or supernaturally with character; it must be developed. Nor are we born with habits—we have to form godly habits on the basis of the new life God has placed within us."[2] And, he admonishes us, "God will not give us good habits or character, and He will not force us to walk correctly before Him. We have to do all that ourselves."[3] Once we take the initiative, we have God's strength to empower us.

Are your present habits—and habits of thought—helping you or hindering your desire to experience wholeness? What is your typical self-talk? Are you telling yourself negative things or positive things? Lies or truth? Are your actions moving you toward being the Christian woman you desire to be, or are they getting in the way?

Instructions

A. Read the following personalized Scriptures. Think about how they compare to your own thoughts and actions.

- God showed his great love for me by sending Christ to die for me, even while I was still a great sinner. (Romans 5:8)
- So there is now no condemnation waiting for me, because I belong to Jesus Christ. For the power of the life-giving Spirit has freed me from the vicious circle of sin and death—and this very power is mine through Jesus Christ. (Romans 8:1 TLB)
- God, you say to me, "For I know the plans I have for you, plans to prosper you and not to harm you; plans to give you a hope and a future." (Jeremiah 29:11)
- I am God's workmanship—his beautiful creation, his work of art—created in Christ Jesus to do good works, which God prepared in advance for me to do. (Ephesians 2:10)
- Since Jesus is my Savior, I am a new creature. The old parts of me are gone, and, guess what! I am a new person! (2 Corinthians 5:17)
- I *can* do all things because of Christ's strength in me! (Philippians 4:13)
- Now, since I have been made right in God's sight by my faith in his promises, I can have real peace with him because of what Jesus has done for me. (Romans 5:1 TLB)

- And I am sure that you, God, who began the good work within me, will keep right on helping me grow in your grace until your task within me is finally finished on that day that Jesus Christ returns! (Philippians 1:6 TLB)
- Because of my faith in Christ, he has brought me into this place of highest privilege where I now stand, and I confidently and joyfully look forward to actually becoming *all* that God has in mind for me to be! (Romans 5:2 TLB)

B. Reflect for a moment on what you've just read. Think about God's desire for your *growth toward beauty and holiness*. Your *complete fulfillment* in him, and him alone. Think, too, about your *true identity* as his daughter, his little girl.

With those things in mind, what are some of the unproductive habits, or habits of thinking, that you are allowing to stand in the way of fully living for Christ? Jot them down here or in your journal:

- _____

- _____

- _____

- _____

- _____

C. Now, pick two of those habits you want to get rid of.
What two *new* positive habits will *replace* them?
Two new positive habits I want to work on are:

1. _____

2. _____

ACTION

What are you willing to do right now to ensure that you will follow through on these desired changes?

(Examples: Tuck a note in my Bible to remind myself to pray about it and ask God's help with it every day • Complete the TED exercise and tape it to my bathroom mirror • Write the new habits on several 3x5 cards and place them in prominent places • Ask an accountability buddy to check in with me at regular intervals)

Wrap-Up

Congratulations! If you just diligently and thoroughly worked your way through those four exercises, give yourself a hug and a trip to the spa! It's not always easy to look deep inside ourselves with honest eyes. I hope you discovered some specific areas where you feel God wants you to grow and blossom with him. It doesn't matter if you discovered lots of things to work on or just a few. What does matter is that you are *moving*—and moving closer to him. That requires a heart that loves him and a willingness to obey.

As we abide with him, we become more aware of his blessings and the sweetness of his fellowship. And over time, as we choose to take action and stay the course with him—trusting, listening, and obeying—we come to realize that he is becoming the perfect answer to our every need.

Involve God in Your Resolve!

Almighty God has the power to change us—on the inside as well as on the outside. You can feel safe putting yourself on his potter's wheel and allowing him to mold you into the perfect woman he created you to be!

> *Abba, you ARE the perfect Man, the perfect Father! What a joy it is to be completely yours! I can crawl up into your lap and cuddle with you anytime I want to. I can feel my small, fragile hand in your strong but gentle grip as we walk along this road of life together. I can lay my head against your chest and feel the fabric of your robe against my cheek. Thank you for revealing to me the lies I wrongly believe and the incorrect thinking that limits my life. I lay them all at your feet. I desire only your pure truth. Thank you that your strength enables me to change*

and grow. And I know that it is you working in me to will and to act according to your good purpose (Philippians 2:13). My greatest desire is to please you.

What else do you want to ask God right now? What else do you want to tell him?

_____

_____

_____

_____

_____

I pray this in the name of your precious Son, Jesus. Amen.

What do you sense he is saying to you right now?

_____

_____

_____

_____

======= Step 12 =======

Put It All Together

He is no fool who gives what he cannot keep to gain that which he cannot lose.

Jim Elliot

Jim Elliot knew the secret.

Let's look at it again: "He is no fool who gives what he cannot keep to gain that which he cannot lose." Do you get it? He was saying, "Lord, I can't keep my life forever anyway, so if I lose it for you and your kingdom, that's okay with me. Whatever I can do for you while I'm down here will last *forever*—it can never be lost!"

Keeping What Can Never Be Lost

In the past eleven chapters we've acknowledged our feelings and our needs. We've discussed our desire for intimacy, love, value, and worth. We've talked about wanting to feel adored and cherished. And we've learned that those deepest needs can only be met fully by the One who loves us eternally.

But here's the truly ironic thing: *in order to get what we really want, we have to give up what we really want.*

- When I finally submit my desires to God with a willingness to do without them, that's when he pours his unending, overflowing love and adoration over me—beyond my wildest expectations.
- When I die to my selfishness and choose to live for him alone, my new self becomes fully alive and begins to live with abundance and exuberance.
- When I willingly give up the things I believe will make me happy in order to obey him, he gives me a joy I've never experienced or dreamed of.
- And when I'm willing to go through discomfort and pain with him in order to obey his will, he rewards me with the sweetest blessings and an indescribable joy.

It's when we die that we begin to truly live.

When we give up everything we can't keep anyway, we gain the treasures we will never lose. When we decide to put him FIRST in our lives, he gives us everything—and more—in return. It's when we die that we begin to truly live.

Butterflies

Did you know that when a butterfly develops inside her chrysalis, most of her caterpillar body actually dies? It has to in order for her to become a butterfly. She goes in as a caterpillar and comes out as a glorious, beautifully winged butterfly. You and I are like butterflies. When we invited Christ into our lives, he clothed us with garments of salvation and arrayed us in robes of righteousness (see Isaiah 61:10). He changed us, *inside* and *out*. We became new creatures in him no longer groveling in the dirt of the world but now free to soar in the beautiful skies of his goodness and love!

So if our old selves have died and we are now glorious creations in Christ, why is it we sometimes find ourselves back on the ground, crawling around in the dirt like that old fuzzy caterpillar? Let's take a look at Peter's story in Matthew 14.

Trust and Obey

It was a cold, blustery night out on the lake. In the small fishing boat the disciples were being buffeted by the waves and the wind. When they saw a man strolling up to their boat, walking on the water, they were terrified. When they realized it was Jesus, Peter said, "Lord, if it's you, tell me to come to you on the water."

Jesus said, "Come."

Then, we are told, Peter climbed out of the boat and walked on the water toward Jesus (Matthew 14:24–30).

Try to put yourself in Peter's sandals. You're in an old wooden boat. It's bobbing in the waves. The mast is creaking with each rocking movement, and the sails are snapping in the wind. The air is brisk and the water is cold and choppy; little whitecaps occasionally lick up over the prow of the boat.

You see Jesus. He says, "Come." You stand up. You step over to the edge and grab the rail. You swing one leg up and over and prepare to step out onto . . . what? What is going to hold you up? What makes you think you can do what Jesus is doing?

Can you imagine the other disciples?

"Are you CRAZY? *Get back inside the boat!!*"

But you lean out over the edge of the vessel, almost to the point of no return. As your weight shifts to your leading foot, you feel the cold water splash against your flesh. But you find that something is holding you up! Imagine your surprise! You swing your other leg up and over and, with a deep breath, let go of the boat. There you are, standing on water!

Your eyes are wide with amazement as you continue to lock eyes with Jesus. Gingerly, you put one foot in front of the other. You're doing it! You're actually walking on water! You feel the icy water sloshing around your toes and ankles, but you don't care. This is an absolute miracle! "Look, Jesus! I'm doing it!"

You're almost there—he's just in reach. Suddenly you become aware of the scene around you.

And you look.

You see the rolling water and the churning waves all about you and you say to yourself, "WHAT AM I DOING? I CAN'T DO THIS!!!"

And you begin to sink.

Acting on Our True Beliefs

Peter *believed* Jesus and *acted* on that belief. But when he took his focus off Jesus and saw the "reality" of the sea around him, he sank. Do you see the secret? As long as you keep your eyes on Jesus—and *believe*—you can "walk on water." The moment you take your eyes off him and look at the waves of the world, the winds of your circumstances, and the depths of your own inadequacies, you begin to sink.

Staying the Course

I still struggle, and I sometimes fail in little ways and big, but Jesus reminds me that as I keep my eyes on him—like Peter on the water—I can, by his strength and grace, have moment-by-moment success. And when I mess up and find myself sinking, all I need to do is cry out like Peter sinking in the waves, *"Lord, save me!"* When I do that, Jesus reaches out and catches me. And in his eyes I see him say, "Why did you doubt me?" (Matthew 14:31). Then once again, I lock my eyes on his and continue my journey.

Only he can fill the holes I've acquired during my life. And that's what this book is all about—learning how to let him give us what it is we really need to feel loved, valued, and cherished beyond our wildest imaginations!

Putting It All Together

Throughout this book we've talked about the steps we need to take to break free of unrealistic beliefs and expectations. And in the last two chapters you had an opportunity to do some honest thinking about the changes you want to make in your own life. Remember, as you choose to act on your decisions, he will work in you to will and to act according to his purpose (Philippians 2:13). He provides the strength and hope you need!

So now let's look at things we can do to keep our eyes on Jesus as we resolve to grow and change.

HOPE

Hope is defined as desiring something with *confident expectation* of its *fulfillment*.[1]

> Those who hope in the LORD
> will renew their strength.
> They will soar on wings like eagles;
> they will run and not grow weary,
> they will walk and not be faint.
>
> Isaiah 40:31

Wow. What promises! Renewed strength. Endurance. Those are the things you can expect from God. Here's a simple formula to keep you on track:

Heed Your Heart, but *Manage* Your Mind
Obey God and His Word
Put Your Trust in God and His Strength
Embrace the Adventure of Living for Christ!

Heed *Your Heart, but* Manage *Your Mind*

1. When you have unruly emotions, remind yourself that although your feelings are real, you don't want them to dictate your thoughts and behaviors. Revisit the worksheet in chapter 3 when you want to better understand your emotions.

2. It's important to be constantly aware of what's going on in your mind—*and* what you put in it! The TED exercise helps to separate the lies from God's truth. That truth will help you renew your mind. Be self-disciplined and stop to consider what you're allowing into your "mental greenhouse."

Consider what you're allowing into your "mental greenhouse."

When you keep your mind filled with what is pure and lovely, it's much easier to keep your focus on the Lord and his desires for you. Christian music, instructional CDs, and books are great for feeding and nourishing your mind.

3. It is critical that you know, understand, and believe your true identity in Christ. You are deeply adored and cherished. You are invited to feast at the abundant banquet table of God's love. You are robed in his glorious righteousness. You are a beautiful, delightful daughter of the King!

4. Recognize the "traps" that keep you from enjoying God's best. Don't give in to even a tiny bit of temptation—that's like stringing big juicy pork chops around your body and then poking a snoozing lion with a pointed stick. In fact, stay away from the zoo altogether.

5. You will fail—that's a fact! But God in his marvelous grace loves you anyway! You can overcome discouragement by reading God's promises. The Psalms are wonderful, as is

spending time with encouraging friends. Also, cut yourself some slack. Remember Proverbs 24:16: "For though a righteous [wo]man falls seven times, [s]he rises again." Instead of beating yourself up, "quietly lay your imperfections before God. . . . And if, at that moment there are some things you cannot understand about his will, simply tell him that you are willing to conform your will to his in all things. And then go on in peace."[2] Persistence is the key.

Obey *God and His Word*

1. Obedience is the only way to real joy. God requires it; you benefit by it. Obedience keeps you out of harm's way and opens the gates to his abundant blessings.

2. Accept that he is God—and you are not! His high standards are expected of you for his high purpose. You'll never hit perfection until he returns for you, but your goal is to be as much like Jesus as you possibly can. Remember, he knows your heart.

3. Continually make choices in light of his Word and his will. And you'll be happier for it.

4. Read and grow to understand him and his Word. In doing so, you can soak in his love and bask in his adoration. As you meditate on and memorize his Word, it becomes a part of your mental arsenal when negative feelings encroach. "I have hidden your word in my heart that I might not sin against you" (Psalm 119:11).

5. Don't put yourself in compromising situations. Once you establish what you truly want, you need to determine how to make it happen and not get sidetracked. An Action Plan follows that will help you to do just that. Trust me, it works!

6. Develop new habits—both with your behaviors and with your thoughts. As you walk through the TED exercise, you'll see the new self-talk you need to integrate into your thinking. The Action Plan will help with your new desired habits.

Put *Your Trust in God and His Strength*

1. Expect great things from a great God! Remember what he tells us in Jeremiah 29:11: "For I know the plans I have for you, plans to prosper you and not to harm you, plans to give you hope and a future." He is fully vested in your future and in your development toward Christlikeness. You have his FULL POWER behind you as you strive to do his will.

2. He knows your every need and your every yearning. He created every cell in your body. He feels every emotion and hears every thought. See Psalm 139, and I suggest you read it frequently. The more you get to know him *intimately*, the more you experience his unconditional and incredible love and adoration for you.

Determine to love him with every fiber of your being, and then hang on for the ride of your life!

3. *You can't do it alone.* You *need* the Holy Spirit and his strength and the support of the body of Christ. Church attendance, a personal quiet time, Bible study, small group participation, and ministry opportunities plug you into the power of the Christian community.

4. God has already won the battle over your enemies. Satan was crushed when Jesus rose from the dead; your whiny old nature was crucified with Jesus, and you yourself no longer live. The world holds no power over him. Since you are "in him," you have the victory too! One small reminder: you need to both *choose* to be victorious and *act* on those victories.

5. Put on the full armor of God. Don't go out without it! I suggest that you read and study Ephesians 6:10–18.

6. Pray without ceasing. Enough said.

Embrace *the Adventure of Living for Christ!*

1. *There is absolutely, unequivocally no greater adventure than living full-out for Christ!* Determine to love him with

every fiber of your being, and then hang on for the ride of your life!

2. *You find what you look for.* When you look for God's hand in your life, you find it. When you anticipate his blessings, you see them. When you expect to sense his love, you do. You need to be in the habit of looking for what I call "kisses from God"—those little blessings that add sweetness to your day.

He hates sin but he loves you!

3. Be quick to repent. Don't hide from God—he hates sin but he loves you! Confess, repent, and get right back into relationship. Don't waste a minute of your incredible life with him.

4. Gratitude and thanksgiving—how can you begin to thank God for all he has done for you? There's just no way to thank him enough! So, be in the habit of thanking him always. Be grateful for everything he has done, is doing, and will do. Thank him in advance for his answers to prayer.

When bad things happen in life—and they will—thank him for how he will use the situation. Thank him for walking with you through it so you don't have to go through it alone. Thank him for what you will learn from it.

5. Live with the realization of his unending abundance—life, love, beauty, opportunity, blessings, grace, mercy, provision.

6. *Practice outrageous joy!* Celebrate your freedom in Christ every single day. Take nothing for granted. "Never be lacking in zeal [ardor, intense enthusiasm], but keep your spiritual fervor [great warmth of emotion, passion], serving the Lord" (Romans 12:11).

Practice outrageous joy!

7. And finally, live *fully* in him! *Know* and *accept* that he loves you deeply, values you enough to send his Son to die for you, and cherishes you beyond belief. He cares about your every dream and desire. He wants you to FEEL adored—and you can if you'll let him adore you. Remember: as you *choose to believe his truth*, it will become *real* for you.

Your Next Step

The next step is up to you. You can either do something or do nothing. My prayer for you, even as I've been writing this book, is that you *choose to do something*. Something that will move you closer to the realization of how much God loves you. Closer to understanding that *HE* is the one who can—and will—fill all the holes and tender places inside. With him our greatest dreams are realized and our deepest needs are satisfied.

I pray that you will choose to fervently live your life for God, knowing that not only does it honor him and please him, but it leads to your complete, unabashed fulfillment. And I pray you will trust him to love you the way he designed you to be loved—*passionately*!

Are you ready?

PERSONAL ACTION PLAN

Awareness—*Knowledge and Understanding*

As you've worked your way through this book, God has been nudging you. What do you feel he is leading you to do? Is he asking you to confront a dark secret sin? Or perhaps confront a wrong belief that is preventing you from living a life based on his truth? Maybe he wants you to break a sinful or negative habit—or develop a new habit that will help you to grow in your walk with him. Write down your thoughts.

_____

_____

_____

Now, pick *one thing* you want to do, develop, or change.

_____

Attitudes—*Perceptions, Beliefs, and Self-Talk (Choice)*

As you prayerfully consider this identified area of your life that God wants you to change, think about how you will need to reframe your thinking in order to be successful. Specifically, how will your attitudes and self-talk need to be changed or modified in order to be consistent with God's Word?

_____

_____

_____

Actions—*New Behaviors and Habits*

God has high expectations for our behaviors. Specifically, how will your actions need to change? What do you want to do *differently* so your behavior in this area is consistent with God's will?

_____

_____

_____

My Commitment and Application

Action Statement: Now, put it all together and write down what it is that you want to do or accomplish. State it as a "SMART Goal": Make it

Specific,
Measurable,
Attainable (remember, you have God's help!),
Relevant to your spiritual growth, and
Time-explicit.

_____

_____

_____

Motives & Benefits: Why is it important to *you* to accomplish this? List as many benefits as you can. What will it look like and feel like when you are successful? How will it impact your fellowship with God? How might it increase your level of peace and joy and freedom?

_____

_____

Timetable: What can you do in the *next thirty days* to accomplish your goal or to make significant progress toward it?

_____

_____

In the *next week*?

_____

_____

Today?

_____

_____

Action Steps: What are some specific steps you will need to take in order to do this?

Specific Action	DTBA*	Done!
•	•	•
•	•	•
•	•	•
•	•	•
•	•	•
•	•	•
•	•	•

*Date To Be Accomplished

Traps, Obstacles, Excuses	Alternatives and Solutions
What are some of the traps or obstacles that might get in the way of your efforts?	*What are the possible solutions for overcoming these traps or obstacles?*
•	•
•	•
•	•
•	•
•	•

Support: Who will support you in this effort? Who will pray for you? Who will hold you accountable? What other help might you need? What books, seminars, materials, and other resources will be helpful or necessary?

Who?/What?	To Do What?	When?
•	•	•
•	•	•
•	•	•

Reminders: What can you do to keep this effort fresh in your mind every day?

Examples: Stick a Post-it note on your computer • Put a 3x5 card on your bathroom mirror • Ask a friend to call you at regular intervals.

Depend on God: Write out a prayer, asking God for his help as you undertake this challenge. Tell him about your desire to honor him with your thoughts and behaviors. Let him know you need his strength and wisdom. Thank him in advance for what he is going to do in your life!

_____

_____

_____

_____

Involve God in Your Resolve!

God is the Filler of all holes! As we grow in our relational intimacy with him, we find the freedom to soar—to live with abundance, abandonment, and a sense of adventure.

Dearest Jesus, when I give up everything I want for you, I get more than I ever dreamed of from you. Let my will and my resolve grow up into the truth of my new identity in you. Let my actions, my words, and my thoughts reflect that belief. In you I have great worth and value. I am your beautiful and precious child—your princess. You desire me, long for me! You love me beyond my wildest visions of being loved. What can I possibly do but love you and obey you in return? Show me your paths of righteousness and give me wisdom to make wise choices. I choose to obey you and to rely on your strength to do what I cannot. Your passion for me gives me freedom to live without fear. I will embrace the adventure of living passionately for you!

What else do you want to ask God right now? What else do you want to tell him?

_____

_____

_____

_____

_____

I pray this in your precious name, Jesus. Amen.

What do you sense he is saying to you right now?

_____

_____

_____

_____

May God bless you
as you join him in this adventure!
And may you come to know, experience,
and embrace his unrestrained love
for *you*—his precious daughter!

Notes

Step 3 Manage Your Feelings

1. Max Lucado, *In the Eye of the Storm* (Nashville: W, 1991), 241.

2. Ibid.

3. Elisabeth Elliot, *Discipline: The Glad Surrender* (Grand Rapids: Revell, 1996), 151.

4. Ibid.

5. Henry Cloud and John Townsend, *Boundaries* (Grand Rapids: Zondervan, 1992).

6. Kathleen Norris, *The Cloister Walk* (New York: Berkley, 1996), 250.

7. John Townsend, *Hiding from Love* (Grand Rapids: Zondervan, 1996), 276.

Step 4 Recognize Common Traps

1. Mari Hanes, *Dreams and Delusions: The Impact of Romantic Fantasy on Women* (New York: Bantam, 1991), 62.

2. Ibid., 91.

3. *Focus on the Family,* "Family Mail", July 1998.

4. "Snared by the Internet," *Today's Christian Woman*, November-December 1997, 88, 90.

5. Shannon Ethridge, *Every Woman's Battle* (Colorado Springs: WaterBrook, 2003), 42.

6. Stephen Arterburn, *Addicted to Love* (Ann Arbor, MI: Servant, 1996), 122.

7. Hanes, *Dreams and Delusions*, 121–22.

Step 5 Accept God's Standards

1. Reference Notes, Luke 15:12, *Life Application Study Bible*, New International Version (NIV)(Wheaton: Tyndale; and Grand Rapids: Zondervan, 1988–1997), 1837.

2. Anne Graham Lotz, *I Saw the Lord: A Wake-Up Call for Your Heart* (Grand Rapids: Zondervan, 2006), 100.

3. Oswald Chambers, *My Utmost for His Highest: An Updated Edition in Today's Language* (Grand Rapids: Discovery House, 1992), September 1.

4. Reference Notes, 1 Peter 1:15–16, *Life Application Study Bible*, NIV, 2258.

5. Jerry Bridges, *The Practice of Godliness* (Colorado Springs: NavPress, 1983, 1996), 121.

6. Cynthia Heald, *Becoming a Woman of Excellence* (Colorado Springs: NavPress, 1986), 92.

7. A. W. Tozer, *The Pursuit of God* (Camp Hill, PA: Christian Publications, 1982), 105–6.

8. Mary Ellen Ashcroft, *Temptations Women Face* (Downers Grove, IL: InterVarsity, 1991), 131.

Step 6 Identify the Opposition

1. Joyce Meyer, *Battlefield of the Mind* (Fenton, MO: Warner Faith, 1995), 15.

2. Ibid.

3. Paul Thigpen, "Our Weaponry," *Discipleship Journal*, May-June 2006, 52.

4. Neil T. Anderson, *The Bondage Breaker* (Eugene, OR: Harvest House, 1990), 67.

5. Reference Notes, Romans 12:2, *Life Application Study Bible*, 2050.

6. Elliot, *Discipline*, 144.

7. Bridges, *Practice of Godliness*, 132 emphasis mine.

8. Chambers, *My Utmost for His Highest*, November 8.

9. John Piper, *A Hunger for God* (Wheaton: Crossway, 1997), 14–15.

10. Ibid., 14.

Step 8 Choose to Follow God

1. Elliot, *Discipline*, 144.

2. Ibid.

3. Chambers, *My Utmost for His Highest*, November 18.

4. Rick Warren, *The Purpose-Driven Life* (Grand Rapids: Zondervan, 2002), 83–84.

5. Chambers, *My Utmost for His Highest*, July 30.

6. Tozer, *Pursuit of God*, 42.

Step 9 Create Godly Habits

1. Adapted from Wilson Learning Worldwide. Used with permission.

2. Chambers, *My Utmost for His Highest*, February 16.

Step 10 Trust God for All Your Needs

1. Sheri Rose Shepherd, *His Princess: Love Letters from Your King* (Sisters, OR: Multnomah Gifts, 2004), 12.

Step 11 Make an Honest Evaluation

1. Robert S. McGee, *Search for Significance* (Nashville: W, 1998), 61.
2. Chambers, *My Utmost for His Highest*, June 15.
3. Ibid., May 10.

Step 12 Put It All Together

1. "Hope," Dictionary/Concordance, *Life Application Study Bible*, 2463.
2. François Fénelon, *Let Go* (Springdale, PA: Whitaker House, 1973), 22.

Note from the Author

God put this book on my heart years ago, and it is amazing to look back and observe how he orchestrated the events that led to the actual writing of it. I have no way of knowing who will read its pages—but God does. So, I'm trusting him to put it into the hands of every woman, counselor, and pastor who will benefit from its message.

Further, I'm praying that as the book is read, hearts and minds will be open to his gentle prodding, and that lives will be changed—from the inside out—forever! If you sense God nudging you, asking you to examine your desires, I want to encourage you to respond to him with an open, submissive, and expectant heart. You won't be disappointed.

My passionate purpose in writing and speaking is to walk with men and women—perhaps women in particular—along the path of experiencing God's deeply personal and transforming love. As we begin to comprehend his desire for intimate relationship, his infinite grace for our frequent stumblings, and his limitless ability to meet our deepest needs and longings, how can we don anything but say "Yes!" to him? And then the real adventure begins!

For information about my speaking ministry, to sign up for my mailing, or to share how God has used this book in your life, please email me at divineromanceinfo@gmail.com. You can also visit my website at www.divine-romance.com.

Dee Bright is a writer, conference speaker, and group facilitator. She has a diverse background in real estate, training, executive leadership, and strategic coaching. An entrepreneur by nature, she has enjoyed working with her own consulting company for over twenty years. She has also been an associate professor at George Fox University. Former director of leadership development at the nine-thousand-member Bayside Covenant Church, Dee lives in Granite Bay, California. Dee has one married daughter, a wonderful son-in-law, two cute grandsons—and one more on the way.

More Bible Studies from ℞ Revell

for individual or group use

DEEPER

For any woman who wants to go deeper spiritually—dig in to Psalm 139 to discover how to live in the reality of God's love. Find out more at deeperbook.com.

BREATHE

Gentle, practical advice on how to make time for what matters most. Includes "breathing" exercises. A MOPS book.

OXYGEN

A devotional that helps you take a deep breath for your soul, incorporating spiritual disciplines into your everyday life. A MOPS book.

Available at your local bookstore

℞ Revell
a division of Baker Publishing Group

Visit divine-romance.com
for more information
and a free leader's guide!

Revell
a division of Baker Publishing Group